Expert Systems and Micros

G L Simons

PUBLISHED BY NCC PUBLICATIONS

British Library Cataloguing in Publication Data

Simons, G. L.
    Expert systems and micros.
    1. Expert systems (Computer science)
    2. Microcomputers
    I. Title
    001.64'25   QA76.9.E96
    ISBN 0-85012-506-5

To some other sorts of expert systems: Christine, Conrad, Corinne, Cornel and Colette.

Geoff Simons

First published in 1985 by:

NCC Publications, The National Computing Centre Limited, Oxford Road, Manchester M1 7ED, England.

Typeset in 11pt Times Roman by UPS Blackburn Limited, 76-80 Northgate, Blackburn, Lancashire, and printed by Hobbs the Printers of Southampton.

ISBN 0-85012-506-5   (NCC Publications)

ISBN 0-470-20277-7   (Halsted Press)

Foreword

by

Dr Matthew Dixon

Manager, Knowledge-Management Systems Group, The National Centre for Information Technology

We are witnessing the emergence – through the expert-systems approach – of useful practical results from the many years of artificial intelligence research. There is also the fast approaching availability of adequate computing power, wherever it is needed, following the arrival of 'super-micros' at acceptably low prices. These developments represent, when viewed together, truly remarkable advances in computer science and technology.

Although each development may be seen as simply an improvement of degree over its forebears, they will together bring a qualitative change in the sophistication and usefulness of computing systems to people of all kinds as they carry out their tasks, whether at work or leisure. Expert-systems technology and other applications of artificial intelligence essentially offer the first real framework for the machine to 'talk up' to us, where in the past we have had to 'talk down' to it – a welcome and timely shift in emphasis.

Geoff Simons' highly readable overview of recent developments and future trends in these two areas, therefore, represents an ideal briefing for those seriously interested in the way computing is going.

It is the task of NCC – the UK national centre for information technology as a whole – to accelerate the sensible transfer of new IT techniques into our industry, business and public administration, and thereby to achieve its strategic objective of promoting the more effective use of computing in Britain. The spread of microcomputers has already produced a situation where more people in this country than ever before need the support, training and advice we can offer to ensure the more effective use of computers. This was seen as desirable when the NCC was created, when machines were numbered in hundreds, and it remains a central NCC objective today.

This book, the latest 'broad-brush' survey of state-of-the-art written by Geoff Simons, exemplifies the kind of helpful information dissemination the Centre can provide at its best. I am sure that this publication will prove as popular and successful as his earlier ones.

Preface

There are many overlapping and converging trends in the international computer industry. Advances in one sector stimulate unexpected developments in another: progress in fabrication technologies, machine architectures, software methods, etc constantly expand the range of computer-application possibilities. Today it is feasible to perform many traditional data processing functions on ever smaller and more economic machines, and it is increasingly possible to equip computers with humanlike capabilities. In this rapidly changing arena, two particular trends can be seen as having great potential for the future: the evolving power of microcomputers and the emergence of artificial intelligence (AI) as a multifaceted commercial reality.

1985 has been dubbed a 'crunch year', a 'year of the great shake-out', for micros and micro suppliers. An increasingly saturated market has led to company collapses, take-overs, and massive price reductions in product lines. The post-1985 micro scene will have a radically changed corporate shape. At the same time, powerful microcomputers will be made available at increasingly economic prices. And 1985 has also been seen as a crucial year for AI. For example, in a spirit typical of current punditry, James Fawcette, editorial director of *InfoWorld*, asks (25 February 1985): 'Will 1985 be the year in which artificial intelligence finally emerges from the ivory towers of academia to become a useful tool?'. In any event, these are important times both for micros and for the rapidly burgeoning world of AI products.

The growing power of microcomputers is signalled in many ways. Applications, for instance, that a few years ago could only run on mainframes can now run on micros (see, for example, the discussion of Micro SAINT models in *Simulation*, January 1985, pp 10-16). And the growing impact of AI products is shown by new commercial packages, new languages and development tools, and new dedicated machines. Moreover, there is increasing convergence between the two developments: the massive processing power that is needed for realisation of some aspects of AI will less and less pose a bar to implementation on micros, and numerous AI-related products are already being developed for microcomputers.

This book charts aspects of these two developments and gives details of their evident convergence. The aim has been to present a 'broad-brush' picture, dealing at times with microcomputer trends, at times with expert systems, and at times with the emergence of micro-based AI facilities. There is some speculation about implications for the future.

Acknowledgements

I am grateful to various companies and individuals for supplying useful information. Particular thanks are due to Tim Johnson (of Ovum Ltd, 14 Penn Road, London N7 9RD) for making available his excellent report, *The Commercial Application of Expert Systems Technology*; and for giving permission to use material from that publication (my Tables 1.3, 1.4 and 6.1, and Figure 3.1 are taken from the report).

Thanks are also due to the following companies and individuals for providing material:

> Expert System Ltd
> ISI Ltd
> Sinclair Research Ltd (Alison Maguire)
> Metacomco (David Sykes)
> Systematics International (Microsystems) Ltd
> Tymshare UK (Nick Lewis)
> TDI Software Ltd
> Microdata UK Ltd
> Southdata Ltd (Peter Laurie)
> Scientific Computers Ltd (G H J Wright)
> Salford University Industrial Centre Ltd (Joyce Cooper)

As usual, NCC staff helped in various ways. I am particularly grateful to Matthew Dixon for his useful comments and for agreeing to write a foreword, to Mike Newman for allowing me access to his files, and to Linda Barrett for assisting with research and production.

Geoff Simons

Contents

Appendix

1 Introduction

GENERAL

Information technology is a rapidly shifting scene: it is perhaps unique, in its pace of development, among modern technologies – and we may speculate on why this should be so. It is certainly true that new computing advances stimulate new insights which in turn generate further progress. And there are various discernible phenomena that are particularly relevant to the themes of the present book. For example, advances in semiconductor technology are continually enlarging the potential of microcomputers, allowing techniques developed for mainframes to percolate downwards to smaller systems. This tendency constantly enlarges the impact of computer technology in industry, commerce, the home and other environments – if only because vastly more potential users have economic access to small computer systems than to large ones.

The phenomenon of *convergence* is also particularly significant in expanding the area of computer influence in the modern world. This effect is evident both at a macro level – for example, where telecommunications and computing converge to become information technology – and at other levels within individual disciplines and activities. Thus computing becomes integrated in scientific research or banking or education, and within computing itself disparate elements (information storage, program semantics, parallel processing, etc) are seen to be increasingly relevant to imaginative computing objectives (knowledge representation, cognitive modelling, the provision of advisory expertise, etc). The move towards 'integrated software' suggests how different computer

applications will increasingly be brought together to provide
multipurpose systems. A convergence of applications – for example, accounting, database, decision support facilities – will characterise many of the new-generation computer systems. And through
increasing user friendliness such systems will become available to
an ever broader range of users.

It is hard to over-emphasise the impact of computers in the
world. We have long known of their use in banks, insurance
companies, in police departments and by military organisations.
Today we are finding out what they can do in factories, the home
and outer space. Their general-purpose nature makes them end-
lessly versatile. Like the human brain they can be applied to a
prodigious realm of activities; and increasingly their tasks have an
intelligent or creative flavour. Today computers can write poems,
short stories and Aesop-type fables; they can compose tunes and
generate harmonisations for existing melodies; they can outperform human games-players, physicians, mathematicians and chemical analysts; and they are providing robots with perceptual and
discriminating intelligence. Mobile robots can now work in lib-
raries, walk across rough terrain, patrol prison perimeters, play
cards and pour drinks.

The growing competence of computer-based systems derives in
part from the spectrum of techniques and applications fashionably
dubbed *Artificial Intelligence*. The idea of 'clever' artefacts is not
new – robots capable of purposeful and intelligent behaviour are
described in Greek mythology, Jewish legend and elsewhere – but
the practical realisation of working systems is peculiar to the
computer age. Artificial Intelligence (AI) is concerned with many
different types of activities – game playing, problem solving,
theorem proving, sensory perception, artistic performance, etc –
but a principal concern is with the provision of advisory or counselling facilities as could be provided by a human expert. Software
providing such facilities are often denoted *expert systems*. These
often embody techniques for solving problems, for manipulating
stored knowledge, for coping with uncertain ('fuzzy') information,
and for explaining to the user how an inference (or some other
activity) is proceeding or a 'conclusion' has been arrived at.

Expert systems are currently a fashionable part of research and commercial activity in the computer industry. They are being 'hyped' as revolutionary solutions to problems in almost every area of human activity, and inevitably the evangelistic excesses and sales pressures are provoking a sceptical backlash (see The AI Controversy, below). There is debate about the character and promise of AI in general and expert systems in particular. However, what is interesting is that expert systems, whatever their precise nature, are now being made available for microcomputers. As we have seen, this will both increase their availability and enlarge their influence.

This chapter explores some of the background to the increasing availability of expert systems. The AI controversy is profiled and aspects of the AI impact are highlighted. Progress in this field depends directly on the activities of interested organisations and the funding that they can attract. Some of the key organisations in this area are indicated and information about investment is included (it is hoped that a further publication later this year will cover such matters in more detail). An introduction to expert systems and to the impact of microcomputers (to be developed in later chapters) is also given. Finally there is brief speculation about the future.

STRUCTURE OF THE BOOK

This chapter establishes a broad framework for what is to follow. Many parallel developments will together influence how expert systems will come to be widely available for users of microcomputers. Chapter 2 highlights aspects of micros that variously explain their current impact and render them more or less suitable for a role in artificial intelligence in general and expert systems in particular. It is also worth reminding ourselves (Chapter 3) of how extensive is the broad spectrum of expert systems, most of which are not available on micros. This will illustrate what advisory and problem-solving facilities will become available for small computer users in the future, if the present trends are maintained. It is inevitable that the large expensive mainframes will continue to exhibit an AI competence that micros will not be able to rival for many years, but we will also see a progressive migration of expert systems, albeit in truncated or simplified forms, from mainframes to smaller and more economic computer systems.

Chapter 4 highlights some features of current expert systems – to indicate elements that should be considered by designers and others considering whether to make expert systems available for micros. This chapter also indicates some of the ways in which expert systems may or may not differ from other types of software. In Chapter 5 we 'name names', focusing on specific expert-systems tools for micros and on some of the companies involved. Whatever the nature of the AI controversy, there are plenty of commercial organisations prepared to argue that they are marketing software products with an AI content. We already see the evolution of a commercial expert-systems sector with distinct related products (LISP machines, dedicated symbolic processing languages, micro 'shells', etc).

It is also worth glancing at the broader implications of developments in expert systems (Chapter 6), particularly as such systems become more widely available to the users of small computer systems. It is one thing for a large corporation to use an expert system for geological prospecting or chemical analysis, but quite another for a medically untrained parent to use an expert system on the home computer to diagnose a disease in an ailing child. There are implications in the increasing availability of expert systems that have not yet been fully addressed. Awareness of such implications could well influence not only how micro-based (and other) expert systems are designed but also what (ethical and legal) liabilities attach to companies marketing products in this field.

THE AI CONTROVERSY

This controversy, sometimes conducted with alarming passion, exists at many levels. One major reason is that the AI phenomenon is perceived as a direct threat to human status (and even sometimes to theological or metaphysical views of the world). At a practical level we find the debate about the actual competence of expert systems. Do they work, as the designers and salesmen claim, or have they been dramatically oversold in a crescendo of 'hype' that even the fast-moving computer industry has rarely witnessed? In the last few (two or three) years AI-based products, often dubbed expert systems, have been represented as every person's magic cure-all, offering easy routes to every problem solution, from how to mend your car to how to educate the backward child. An AI solution has even been offered as a means to greater international security. Current computer-based military systems, it is argued, are unreliable because they are not run by intelligent software: a new-generation AI 'fix' is the answer – people will know what is happening because the computers will tell them. Complex computer-based decision-making, so the argument runs, will no longer be opaque to human understanding. So expert and related systems will develop the potential of the dull-witted infant, diagnose those troublesome diseases, lever the United States into world supremacy (Feigenbaum and McCorduck, 1984), and save the world from nuclear catastrophe. When a proliferation of such claims are made, it is easy to sustain the charge that expert systems are being oversold.

What has happened is that, partly impelled by the Japanese fifth-generation initiative, a variety of AI techniques are now being incorporated in commercial products. Most of these techniques have been around for some time and there is debate about their real status as AI components. According to some estimates, AI has been pursued for at least thirty years, but during most of that period by under-funded enthusiasts on the fringes of the computer industry. Today there is increased willingness to recognise at least some of the claims of the AI fraternity – and a commercial bandwagon, of questionable worth, is one consequence.

There are signs that even the specialist AI community, usually ignored and sometimes ridiculed for two decades or more, concedes that expert systems have been oversold. A main worry is that the new funding will quickly dry up in the wake of the inevitable backlash. Media hype will cause the public, company managements and governments to have unreasonable expectations. Research into expert systems will not be able to deliver the goods, and whatever advances are made will necessarily be seen as disappointing – so subsequent funding will be affected. Thus one observer (Anderson, 1984) comments: 'The extent of the belief that AI has been overplayed is surprising. It comes from the ranks of all the major players – computer scientists, academics, industry analysts, company executives and AI researchers themselves'. And reference is made to comments by Lewis Branscombe, chief scientist at IBM, in a keynote address at a late-1984 meeting of the Association for Computing Machinery (ACM). This observer spoke of the 'extravagant statements' that had become a source of concern. Government leaders 'who control the support so vital for research progress' could become disenchanted. In a similar vein Professor John McCarthy, one of the early AI pioneers, wonders whether the present technology can justify the present industry being built upon it ('I sure would like to see more applications that are certified to be not experimental any more but in genuine use').

Existing expert systems are often seen to be very limited. It is felt that they do not model the multiple levels of reasoning that are found in human beings. Thomas Rindfleisch, director of the Heuristic Programming Project at Stanford, has emphasised that the current theories that underlie AI are at a very rudimentary stage, just as Jay Tenenbaum, director of the Fairchild Laboratory for Artificial Intelligence, has stressed that expert systems need to be more flexible in their application potential ('these systems are all hand tailored'). One problem is that there are relatively few real AI experts, though many companies are keen to boast AI features in their products.

Herbert Grosch, former IBM scientist (quoted by Anderson), told the ACM conference: 'The emperor – whether talking about the fifth generation or AI – is stark naked from the ankles up. From the ankles down the emperor is wearing a well worn and heavily-gilded pair of shoes called expert systems'. These, he points out, are useful but they have been around for more than thirty years. In one view, modern researchers have simply invented a new vocabulary. Such terms as 'artificial intelligence', 'knowledge base' and 'expert system' are, it is proposed, emotive and pretentious, signalling seeming technological advances which in reality have not occurred. S Jerrold Kaplan, AI expert at Teknowledge, has suggested that if artificial intelligence had been called *symbolic programming* there would have been less popular interest. The emotive appeal of AI may have proved sufficient to attract funds but this may be counterproductive.

The annual conference of the American Association of Artificial Intelligence (AAAI), held in Texas in August 1984, revealed similar disquiet about the image of AI. John McDermott, of Carnegie-Mellon, suggested that there were exaggerated expectations about the potential of AI. It may be imagined, for instance, that artificial intelligence can solve any problem, that any AI development is necessarily successful, and that 'quick and dirty' AI laboratories can be effective. Roger Schank, of Yale, suggested that companies were into AI, but with 'second-order' people. In consequence, AI had become commercial before its time. Again there is the danger that business will become disenchanted, with consequent effects on investment policies. A 1960s precedent is how funding evaporated when commercial results from research into computer-aided language translation were slow to emerge.

The current media hype of expert systems has many aspects. In part it represents the journalistic search for novelty; and then, as we have seen, there is the manipulation of a new vocabulary by committed specialists in order to attract company and government interest, and subsequent funding. And underlying all the publicity is the perennial titillation by the notion that at last computers are learning to think like human beings. But what is the reality? What is the commercial status of available expert systems? There are many such products (see Chapter 3), but how useful are available systems to businessmen and factory managers who are not in the least interested in symbolic programming or nonmonotonic logic but who simply want effective solutions to practical problems?

In one view (for example, Martins, 1984), expert systems are much less successful than the media hype suggests. Moreover they incur high development costs and are expensive to run when they are eventually made available. In addition it seems difficult to develop expert systems for any but the simplest applications, and the available shells (the expert-system tools that can in principle be adapted to a wide range of different problems) have many limitations. Hence Martins declares : 'For the most part, current off-the-shelf expert-systems tools . . . cost too much, are poorly supported, lack adequate documentation, are hard to use, yield very inefficient programs, and seem to have sharply limited applicability to complex, real-world problems'. In such circumstances we would not be surprised to see adverse effects on investment and company commitment, and there are already signs that some expert-systems houses face difficulties ('some . . . are thrashing about in a desperate search for new survival strategies').

Another point, linked to the notion of a bogus and seductive vocabulary, is the extent to which the expert-systems technology is *original*. Have established ideas simply been relabelled or is there a genuine technological breakthrough that represents a new dimension in computer competence? It is worth summarising key observations made by Martins (1984):

— *production rules*, a key feature of expert systems, are not new. They were devised by logicians in the 1920s, borrowed by linguists in the 1950s, by cognitive psychologists in the 1960s, and later by AI workers;

— a methodology equivalent to the *if* (conditions) *then* (actions) was invented in the 1960s and called 'decision-table programming';

— the *inference engine*, another common expert-systems feature, is simply the equivalent of the common interpreter, a familiar element in versions of Lisp, Prolog and BASIC.

Such lack of originality in key expert-systems features may not constitute a real drawback. It may be that traditional computer notions can be combined to produce unusual and worthwhile results. But critics suggest that this is far from the case with expert systems. It is alleged that the only successful applications are simple ones, and that expert-systems code is often difficult to understand, debug and maintain. Moreover the appearance of transparency in rule-based programs may be held to be illusory: the deceptive clarity quickly vanishes when the rules proliferate. And even the related profession of 'knowledge engineering' invites criticism (the knowledge engineer derives expertise from human specialists to incorporate in knowledge-based systems).

There is of course a sense in which traditional programmers and systems analysts have always investigated human expertise to allow programs to be written. The analyst, for example, will often be required to interview the people on the job to see how best the task can be programmed. Do knowledge engineers do more than this? AI buffs would say so, though critics would be sceptical. Hence Martins comments: 'There is no credible evidence that knowledge engineers have advanced our understanding or mastery of the problems of knowledge acquisition, representation, or use'. It may even be the case that the efforts of the knowledge engineers to produce effective programs are impeded by their simplistic methods. At the same time the knowledge engineers are portrayed as heralds of new-generation systems, an effective bridge between traditional programming and truly intelligent machines.

In summary, the critics of expert-systems hype argue that such systems are only effective for relatively simple problem domains, and in any case the systems do not rely on revolutionary new techniques but on proven programming methods. Where a revolutionary or breakthrough image is purveyed, we can quickly discern exaggerated claims and the manipulation of an emotive vocabulary.

The danger of the criticism is that it will discourage people from recognising the advances that have been made. We will see that expert systems are working usefully on a day-to-day basis, though claims for their abilities are often excessive, particularly in the popular press. There is still a considerable commitment, on the part of governments and companies, to the value of AI research. In 1983, European governments and other organisations spent about £20 million in this field; in 1984 the figure rose to around £330 million. And there are plenty of observers to set against Grosch and Martins. Thus Ian Mackintosh, head of consultants Mackintosh International, suggests that AI 'is an inevitable next step in the onward march of technology and there is nothing that will stop it'. In such a view there is no doubting the technical and economic feasibility of the new ideas. Roger Foster, managing director of Applied Computer Techniques, reckons that artificial intelligence is here to stay ('I don't think it's a one-day wonder').

There is frequent reference, in the technical and trade literature, to the confusion in the present situation. In the late-1970s the Japanese startled the rest of the industrial world by announcing their fifth-generation plans (a fifth-generation computer was to be designed by around 1990). The alarm occasioned by this declaration stimulated a rapid response in the UK, Europe and elsewhere. The Alvey programme in Britain was one result (see below). But, underlying the various initiatives, doubts were evident. Was the government involvement sufficient? Excessive? And perhaps the basic philosophy behind fifth-generation systems was ill-conceived. Was it really practical to launch a research programme to develop intelligent machines? We do not need to rehearse the familiar arguments against artificial intelligence (see, for example, Simons, 1984, pp 53-58). It is enough to remark that emotional and intellectual doubts still surround the whole AI enterprise – as shown, for example, in the recent BBC Reith lectures* given by John Searle, professor of philosophy at the University of California, Berkeley. When such general doubts attend the basic AI posture, it is hardly surprising that expert systems are viewed with scepticism.

We have seen that the AI controversy exists at many levels. Specific AI-related products, eg expert systems, are criticised in various ways (Schank has even declared that expert systems in the current marketplace contain no AI), and broad hostility can be evoked against the possibility of machine intelligence *per se*. The answer to the sceptics will consist in demonstrating effective systems, computer-based facilities that will manifest evident intelligence in various roles. Some observers claim that this has already been achieved. In any event the growing impact of AI is clear.

THE AI IMPACT
General
The impact of artificial intelligence, hyped or not, is already evident in commerce, industry, schools, the military arena, etc. Practical applications, involving expert systems and other types of software, are now available on a commercial basis. We have seen suggestions that many of the claims are exaggerated, and there is evident confusion in the marketplace. At the same time this is a rapidly changing situation. There is enough committed funding to guarantee technological progress, though there is debate about precisely what will be achieved.

The field of expert systems is marked by a proliferation of applications (see Chapter 3) though they are not all equally impressive. Some products which appear to mimic human competence are in fact on the fringes of artificial intelligence: they do not embody the heuristic and other techniques that characterise AI

---

* We cannot explore these points here. Those interested should consult the Searle paper in Hofstadter and Dennett (1982), to which Hofstadter comments are appended.

proper, yet make claims that suggest a capacity for humanlike behaviour. Other products seemingly exhibit a facility for intelligent discrimination but rely on traditional software devices that have been available for many years. Other systems are in development, promising much but, to date, yielding little. For example, research into voice-controlled equipment, an AI concern, is proceeding on several fronts.

The Alvey directorate has supported research into a voice-operated word processor, and work is also under way on voice-controlled navigation and radio gear for future fighter aircraft. Another Alvey-funded initiative is concerned with linking an expert system with telephone inquiry services incorporating speech recognition and synthesis: an automatic train-timetable service will be accessed by telephone. The expert system will be able to 'understand' questions (ie perform an effective semantic analysis) and answer them. And such a facility may not be impeded by foreign languages. Research is being carried out to establish a translating telephone. In one implementation, it would be possible to talk to someone in another country, even if the two people did not understand each other's languages. The telephone would translate the words in transmission. The head of NEC, Dr Kobayashi (interviewed by Rex Malik, 1984), is supporting just such a project.

Much of the AI impact derives from the impetus given to fifth-generation research by the Japanese (for example, see Simons, 1983). From the initial Japanese announcements in the late-1970s, AI research attracted new interest and unprecedented levels of investment. It is already true that many large companies – DEC, Shell, ICI, Unilever, etc – are using expert systems in day-to-day problem solving. This has shown that some of the early criticisms of AI were unfounded. For example, it was suggested – by Sir James Lighthill (in his 1973 *Report on Artificial Intelligence*) and others – that AI was impossible because of the combinatorial explosion: too many options would need to be explored in any AI program. However there are now effective search strategies, involving heuristic and other methods, to overcome this problem. Bayesian statistics, for example, can be exploited to assign probabilities to options in conditions of uncertainty.

The new awareness of AI should be set against its actual history. Artificial intelligence has had a fictional presence for more than 3000 years, and the theoretical systems for logic, syntax and knowledge representation can be traced to the Ancient Greeks. The syllogisms of Aristotle have an uncanny resemblance to the production rules of modern expert systems. It is worth reminding ourselves of some of the historical landmarks on the route to present-day AI activity and concern (see Table 1.1).

Some of the early successes of expert systems and related products were not sufficient to stimulate international interest and attract large investment. The much-cited Prospector system gained immortality by finding molybdenum where human geologists said there was none, showing that expert systems could be commercially important. Dendral achieved various successes in interpreting mass spectrometry data, and the medical-diagnosis systems (MYCIN and others) managed a degree of competence at least equal to that of most human physicians. But despite such early successes it was not until the 1980s that expert systems and other AI-related products exploded upon the scene. Thus Randall Davis, a professor of artificial intelligence at the Massachusetts Institute of Technology, can observe: 'It's ironic. Three years ago, AI was considered flaky. Now it's hot, and everyone wants in'. And this is seen as a highly commercial situation. 'It's a gold rush' declares Larry Geisel, head of Carnegie Group, a new AI company started by four Carnegie-Mellon researchers. A 1984 report in *Businessweek* (9 July) notes that in the previous three years, venture capitalists in the United States had poured more than $100 million into some forty small firms intent on deriving commercial benefits from AI. And massive research into artificial intelligence has been initiated by more than thirty of the largest US corporations – ITT, General Electric, Schlumberger, Hughes Aircraft, FMC, Litton, etc.

The AI impact, despite the frequent negative sounds heard in the AI controversy (see above), is discernible in the changing shape of the computer marketplace, in the funding policies of governments and companies, and in the popular and technical views of what the computer industry is likely to achieve in the years ahead. There is also a discernible impact on how particular types of

Date	Innovation
1854	George Boole develops the symbolic logic that would later prove useful in computer design
1936	Alan Turing develops the general 'Turing Machine', basic to the theory of computing
1943	Colossus, first electronic computer, developed at Bletchley
1956	John McCarthy, later to invent Lisp language, coins the phrase 'artificial intelligence'
1957	Newell, Shaw and Simon develop the General Problem Solver, a key AI landmark
1964	First versions of Dendral, early expert system, announced
1971	First microprocessor, the Intel 4004, launched
1972	Unimation starts to make robots as sole product
1972	Terry Winograd designs SHRDLU programs to understand natural language
1973	Threshold Inc introduce first speech-recognition system
1973	The (Sir James) Lighthill Report discourages UK AI research
1979	Japan announces fifth-generation plans
1982	Japan launches fifth-generation programme
1983	Alvey programme (UK) and Esprit programme (Europe) launched as response to Japanese initiatives
1984	Proliferation of software products claiming AI content; debate about worth of expert system shells, etc
1991?	First fifth-generation systems incorporating expert systems and other AI features

Table 1.1 Landmarks on the Route to AI

software are coming to be regarded. There is a candid suggestion, explicit in much of the new vocabulary, that computer software is viewed as exhibiting *mental* properties. If vocabulary were all that mattered, the AI controversy would be at an end.

Software

There is an obvious sense in which much of the rest of this book is about software. Expert systems are programs of great diversity (see Chapter 3) and with characteristic features (see Chapter 4). The requirements of expert systems have implications for hardware (for example, in relation to cycle times, storage capacity, interface provisions, etc) but attention to expert systems usually involves consideration of software possibilities. In this section, without focusing specifically on expert systems, certain software products are highlighted, partly to indicate how an emerging vocabulary is influencing an ethos in which computer programs are supposed to mimic mental activities.

In one 'somewhat revolutionary software category' (Haner, 1984), *mindware* allows users to exploit the personal computer as an 'information appliance'. This means that thoughts and ideas can be set down in a random order and then sequenced by keyword or similar lists. The ambitious aim is to extend the thought processes of the user. Mindware is depicted as spreadsheets for ideas, perfect for writers, business users and students 'who seek to improve their ability to think, create, plan and solve problems'. The category includes:

— *Thinktank* (from Living Videotext Inc), an idea processor to aid the outlining process by creating traditional conceptual outlines and using major topic headings and indented subtopics;

— *Brainstormer* (from Softpath Systems), devised to propose solutions to sales problems. For example, why are sales dropping? Brainstormer prompts the user to ask relevant questions;

— *The Idea Processor* (from Idea Ware Inc), a thought processor that separates the brainstorming and thought-collection processes to aid the manipulation of ideas;

— *Maxthink* (from Maxthink Inc), built around sixty thought-processing modules to expand the creative and decision-making capabilities of the user.

Mindware has also been dubbed 'software for the brain'. This is a category that will develop rapidly, encouraging enhanced human/computer interaction, as artificial-intelligence techniques become more widely used.

Another software innovation, inevitably termed 'revolutionary', is *Brainstorm* (not to be confused with Brainstormer) from Caxton Software. This package (see, for example, Bidmead, 1984; Sanders, 1984) is supposed to help with the creative side of writing by using the common software device called 'information hiding'. The basic notion is that ideas in a large project are often organised hierarchically to render them manageable. Each level can be considered independently without the user being distracted by what is happening elsewhere.

Brainstorm, essentially a fancy word-processing package, has a generalised applicability. David Tebbutt, Caxton's Director (and with Mike Liardet a co-author of Brainstorm), observes: 'We use it for everything: project planning, program design, document drafting – in fact, whenever there is a need to organise creative thoughts and turn them into practical propositions'.

The mindware sector is related to expert systems, and not only by an increasingly common 'mental' vocabulary. In both areas we find efforts to manipulate text, to handle propositions in a creative way to yield useful suggestions and conclusions. The COPE package, developed by Bath Software Research in conjunction with the University of Bath, is yet another ideas processor. Again the system is promoted as being able to help with investment decision making, policy making and creative thinking. It has been used by senior managers in various environments:

— in a major nationalised industry to help with corporate planning;

— in a UK oil company to assist in the Operational Research Department;

— in the UK publishing industry to help with the redesign of a magazine and for management training;

— in the furniture and timber industries to evaluate machine purchase decisions;

— in major national charities and local government departments to aid the generation of new policies and new ways of working;

— in a software house to assist in the design of a new software package.

COPE operates by helping a decision-maker to build a model of the problem. Here the model is based on the technique of cognitive mapping, a pictorial approach to highlighting the key elements in a problem and the way they influence each other. The system – available in versions for mainframes, minis and micros – can generate a textual report or illustrate conclusions in the form of a map. COPE, in common with the other emerging ideas processors, illustrates an important feature of modern software evolution – that systems are developing to handle concepts, a key element in artificial intelligence.

The 'mental imagery' of AI-related software is further illustrated by the use of such terms as 'reasoning', 'conclusion drawing' and 'inference making' to denote behaviour in modern systems. For example, the Institute of New Generation Computer Technology (ICOT) of Japan has recently (late-1984) demonstrated software designed to draw inferences from separate pieces of information. The software uses situation semantics to go beyond a study of the inherent meaning in single sentences to consider the inferences to be drawn from separate statements considered together. In such a fashion, software is emerging to mimic what has always been regarded as an important capacity in human thinking.

Other software, often serving an advisory or counselling purpose, has been termed 'psychological' (see, for example, Neimark 1984; Caruso, 1984). Psychological (or 'psych-out') software can, for instance, operate as a plug-in consultant to explore the behaviour and attitudes of business associates and to map out strategies for conducting negotiations and managing staff. This type of software was first evident six or seven years ago, and in late-1984 Human Edge Software, a leading manufacturer, reckoned that the market would reach $73 million by 1987.

The claims for software in this sector are seen as extravagant by some observers. What do we make of suggestions that psych-out software can help to rehabilitate the brain-damaged, make effective psychiatric evaluations, improve your memory, and help you to avoid stress? Can software really be useful in developing personality profiles, assessing the extent of neuronal damage, interpreting dreams, and analysing the motivations of colleagues and competitors? The programs are usually very limited. AI enthusiast Marvin Minsky admits that even the best psychological programs 'are not very deep', and the worst are likely not only to be shallow but also dangerous in the wrong hands. Gaines Thomas, a California psychologist, expresses the well-known fact: people tend to 'over-rely on a computerised report and . . . to take it as gospel'. This is a problem that needs discussion in the context of expert systems (see Chapter 6).

Psychological software aims to perform many of the tasks that are traditionally carried out by psychologists, managers, financial analysts and other human experts. The package names (Brainstormer, Thinktank, Mind-Prober, etc) signal the involvement with intellectual or psychological activities, and many of the company names (Thoughtware, Psych Systems, Computer Thought, Psycomp, etc) convey the same message. The age of mindware has arrived and this is one of the factors that is influencing the technological and commercial climate in which expert systems will evolve.

Commercial

A recent Arthur D Little Inc study (cited by Sullivan, 1984) has forecast that the market for artificial intelligence – including hardware, software and services – would reach $5 billion to $10 billion by 1990. And within five years, this market will grow to between $30 billion and $70 billion. The study predicts that by the end of the century, the market will reach the $50 billion to $110 billion range, and constitute a remarkable 20% of the total computer industry market. The caveats of the sceptics, it seems, are doing little to dent the optimism with which the commercial world views the likely growth in the volume of AI-related products.

It is already obvious that many expert systems and other products claiming 'to contain AI' are flowing onto the market. An article in *Businessweek* (9 July 1984) proclaims: 'Suddenly, optimistic analysts are predicting that AI will become a multibillion-dollar annual business well within a decade'. And it is suggested that the market for expert and related systems products will explode from about $20 million in 1984 to around $2.5 billion by 1993. There is also parallel market growth in the software that allows users to communicate in natural language (English, Japanese, Russian, etc) with expert systems and conventional computer programs. This associated market, one among several, is itself expected to reach about $1.8 billion annually by 1993.

One reason for such 'bullish' predictions is that market analysts expect expert systems to broaden the use of computers throughout their current areas of application, as well as moving computers into new markets. When this growth potential becomes widely perceived, it will become easier for both new and established AI-related companies to attract investment (see Investment and Funding, below). Of course the predictions may be unsound. We have already noted that the 'overselling' of expert systems may generate a backlash that will cause funding to evaporate. But on current evidence it seems likely that there will be a rapid growth in commercial AI in the years ahead.

Social

The impact of artificial intelligence on society will be multifaceted. To an extent, AI will simply enlarge the already manifest impact of traditional computing. There will, for example, be consequences for employment (particularly in the 'thinking professions'), for privacy, government surveillance and other human-rights areas. There will be effects in such caring professions as education and medicine. And in addition there may be consequences for areas of human experience as yet relatively untouched by traditional computing. There may be effects on social intercourse, human self-image, and how life in general is perceived. There may come a time when intelligent computers are indisputably the best games players, confidants, advisors and conversationalists. How will we react? (More is said about this in Chapter 6.)

ORGANISATIONS INTO AI

General

Many organisations are now involved in AI research and the marketing of commercial products. There is growing investment on the part of both governments and companies (see below), and well-defined research programmes are emerging in universities throughout the developed world. There is still debate about the quality of the research and the resulting products, but it is hard to see the present worldwide AI momentum failing to yield an impressive range of new hardware, software and services. This development will have profound consequences for the shape of the computer industry, a growing sector of which will be expert systems for mainframes, minis and microcomputers.

Alvey

In February 1982, Kenneth Baker, the then Minister for Information Technology, announced intentions to set up a Group to study a research programme involving a collaborative effort by the UK government, industry and universities with the aim of developing information-technology products. The Group came to be headed by John Alvey, senior director of technology at British Telecom. The resulting Report (see summary in Appendix 2) is a key document signifying UK awareness of the need for a more active involvement – on the part of government, companies and universities – in Information Technology.

By 1985 about 120 projects, involving research spending of some £180 million, had been initiated (one listing of these is given by Green-Armytage, 1984; and see also the survey, 'Alvey's Joint Approach' in *Engineering*, January 1985, and the Alvey 84 Annual Report). The projects have been divided into eight categories:

— Very Large Scale Integration;

— VLSI – Architecture;

— VLSI – CAD;

— Software Engineering;

— Intelligent Knowledge-Based Systems;

— Man-Machine Interface;

— Large Demonstrators;

— Infrastructure and Communications.

Virtually all the projects listed under these heads are relevant, directly or indirectly, to the development of AI products, including expert systems. Projects specifically devoted to knowledge-based systems are shown in Table 1.2.

International Scene

The Japanese announcement of its fifth-generation plans had an immediate impact on the rest of the industrial world. Some observers likened the impact to that caused by the Soviet Union's launch of the first artificial satellite more than a quarter of a century earlier. Today in the West there are plenty of national and individual company activities in the general field of fifth-generation, AI and expert systems but (it is still true that) Japan holds the initiative in many areas.

In Japan the programme is focused on the Institute for New Generation Computer Technology (ICOT) funded to the tune of $24 million for the 1984-85 financial year. ICOT maintains up to forty researchers seconded by the companies participating in the project. A much larger number of researchers are active in the laboratories of the participating companies. MITI (the Ministry of Trade and Industry), NTT (the telephone company) and the eight leading Japanese firms are all contributing to the work of ICOT. In one estimate (by Bob Muller of SPL), there were about 300 people involved in the fifth-generation project by mid-1983.

ICOT has proposed research according to a three-phase plan.

— the first phase (1982 to 1985) was intended to develop basic technology;

— the second (1985 to 1989) is intended to develop sub-systems;

— the third (1989 to 1992) is intended to end with the

development of a complete system that can be transferred to industry for production.

Project	Company	University
Dictionary, analyser for English language processing	Acorn	Edinburgh, East Anglia
IKBS system architecture using control flow	?	Reading
Intelligent help file finder	SDL	Sussex
Procurement for 10 GEC Series 63 computers	GEC	
Framework for specification of information systems	STL	Imperial
Extraction of 3D structure in low-level vision	GEC	Sussex
Automatic natural language research	Acorn	Cambridge
Study for design of a Prolog machine	Cambridge Consultants, Logic Programming Assoc	
Knowledge engineering assistant for constructing fault diagnosis systems	BT	OU
Computational grammar of English	Acorn	Cambridge
Read/write Japanese without knowing it	ICL	UMIST, Sheffield
Software house staff allocation expert system	John Bell	Exeter
Natural language generation from plans	BT	Sussex
Tools for development of logic programs		Imperial
Applications of functional closures	Acorn	Bath
3D surface representation from stereoscopic lines	GEC, IBM	Sheffield, Edinburgh
Study of computational approach to text processing		Edinburgh
Enhancement to Poplog expert systems development environment	SDL	Sussex
Flexible toolkit for building expert systems	GEC	Edinburgh
Spatio-temporal processing and optical flow for computer vision	GEC, BAe, Plessey	QMC
IKBS applications for simulation for avionics tactical decision aids	Schlumberger, Rediffusion, Smiths	
Logic front ends for large software systems	NAG	Imperial

Table 1.2   IKBS Projects in Alvey Programme

The overall ICOT programme can be seen as an attempt to develop a total hardware and software environment for the production and operation of expert systems and other AI-related applications. The programme will directly impact on the development of expert systems for mainframes, minis and microcomputers. However it has also been emphasised (eg by Johnson, 1984) that the development of expert systems accounts for a relatively small part of the whole project. We may expect ICOT research to feed into individual companies which may then generate expert systems and related products. At the same time the companies will fund their own research programmes. There are already a number of expert systems developed for practical purposes by Japanese companies.

The NEC Corporation has produced an expert system, Wirex, that aids VLSI chip design by cutting layout time in half. Daniel Bobrow, a research fellow at the Intelligent Systems Laboratory of the Xerox Palo Alto Research Centre, has commented: 'Corporations in Japan seem to be focusing on internally generated expert systems that deal with well-understood problems . . . they are installing expert systems in real environments where there are real problems'. Wirex is seen as a typical example of such systems. Details of this design facility were given at the recent International Conference on Fifth Generation Computer Systems held in Tokyo and sponsored by ICOT (see Murtha, 1985).

Another leading Japanese company has been working with ICOT on a Prolog-based expert system for hardware logic design (resulting patents will be held by MITI and made available to Japanese firms). The success of the system (Takao Uehara, deputy manager of Fujitsu's software laboratory in Kawasaki, has noted: 'We are very satisfied with the preliminary results') has encouraged the company to develop expert system tools for outside customers. However it is still thought that Japan trails the US in expert systems development. Hitachi, for example, with a 1984 R & D budget of $941 million, only began to explore expert systems in 1981, a couple of decades behind many American firms. Today Hitachi is funding more than a dozen knowledge engineering research projects.

The Japanese, with pragmatic intent, often design expert systems to link with Fortran subroutines whereas most US applications are developed for dedicated Lisp machines. The tendency of the Japanese researchers to restrict development to practical in-house applications has also retarded the development of the Japanese market, a situation that is rapidly changing as systems are developed for external customers.

The main US government response to the Japanese challenge has come from the Defence Advanced Research Projects Agency (DARPA) of the Department of Defence. The US appears not to be keen on coordinated national research efforts that do not have military connections. In November 1983, DARPA proposed a 'strategic computing' programme for new-generation systems. The aim was to create 'a broad base of machine intelligence technology for application to critical defence problems'. The 10-year programme, to cost $600 million in the first five years, began with fiscal 1984 (ie from 1st July 1984). A central aim is to develop expert systems and other AI products (for example, for image recognition and natural language interfaces) for specific military purposes.

The establishment of 5 to 10 new research communities is envisaged to focus on applications, with 10 new computing technology communities. Each community is expected to involve at least a hundred people, leading to annual costs of around $150 million (a total of 1500 researchers costing $100,000 each). It is expected that the DARPA programme will greatly encourage the rapid development of AI-linked products, including expert systems. The programme, the Strategic Computing Initiative (SCI), will involve coordination with many other US government bodies. DARPA has requested $95 million for fiscal year 1985, a request already authorised by the House and Senate. (The DARPA plans are discussed in some detail by Schatz and Verity, 1984.)

In addition to DARPA, other lead organisations in the US are the Microelectronics and Computer Technology Corporation (MCC) and the Semiconductor Research Cooperative (SRC). Both DARPA and MCC (a consortium of 18 electronics companies) are supported by the SRC (an industry-academia collaborative) and the Microelectronics Centre of North Carolina (MCNC) (a consortium of state, government and academic bodies).

A number of universities – for example, the University of Minnesota and the Stanford University Centre for Integrated Systems (CIS) – have formed research cooperatives. (Details of these various organisations are given in Highberger and Edson, 1984; and in Quinn, 1984.)

In Europe the main response to the Japanese initiative is the Esprit programme, represented as a larger, looser version of Alvey. In this connection the Commission of the European Community is providing $620 million to provide 50% funding to collaborative R & D projects in five areas: microelectronics, software technology, advanced information technology, office systems and computer integrated manufacture. One aim is for each project to include participation from companies in at least two member countries of the European Economic Community.

Expert systems research is included in the *advanced information technology* topic. An initial contract, worth $900,000 and shared between the Polytechnic of the South Bank (London), Scicon and the University of Amsterdam, was to develop a methodology for the design of expert systems. Another contract, worth $450,000, required Scicon, its German sister company, the Belgian Institute of Management and the German Frauenhofer Institute to develop tools for building expert systems with natural language interfaces. Johnson (1984) suggests that such consortia have rarely produced valuable direct results in the past.

Another European initiative is the plan formulated by ICL, Siemens and Compagnie de Machines Bull to establish a joint advanced research institute. The aim is for the three leading indigenous European mainframe manufacturers to share the costs of an institute devoted to developing software and networking techniques for knowledge-based systems. The intention is to build up to about fifty researchers within two years. The scheme is independent of Esprit and is likely to have considerable commercial impact.

In the UK, in addition to the Alvey programme, there are various initiatives worth mentioning. A European artificial intelligence centre is being developed at Cambridge University by the US research organisation, SRI International. SRI and Cambridge will collaborate on research, each contributing staff. (The American company claims to employ at least 20% of North America's AI researchers.)

Expert systems research is also being funded by the GLC-supported Greater London Enterprise Board. This follows the establishment of a new centre, the London New Technology Network, created to channel funds into projects deemed to be socially useful. Already work is under way on expert systems to enable family doctors to cope with a wide range of serious conditions outside their experience. For example, it is expected that GPs will soon be supplied with micro-based packages to aid the treatment of diabetes. This work has involved medical consultants at St Thomas's hospital, London, and use has been made of the APES expert system shell (from Imperial College) running under Unix on a Fortune micro. Other expert system projects promoted by the Network involve Queen Mary College and the Polytechnic of Central London.

Another UK development is the Turing Institute, formerly Edinburgh University's Machine Intelligence Research Unit, now emerging as a non-profit distributing company to be run by Donald Michie at Strathclyde University. The institute will provide post-graduate teaching, and on the industrial side a small group of companies are paying subscriptions. Their payments provide the firms with cut-price services, including computing facilities, software, technical reports, consultancy and seminars. One key objective is effective industrial/academic cross-fertilisation: the companies learn about AI techniques, and the institute can use seconded staff and is forced to address real-world problems.

The international AI scene is multifaceted; specific national and individual-company plans sometimes deriving from traditional or embryonic activities and sometimes being created in a research vacuum. Governments, companies and universities throughout the developed world (both East and West) are now showing an unprecedented commitment to the work of AI specialists. It is easy to argue that the impact of AI-related systems has been oversold. If this circumstance causes a backlash, the most damaging impact will be on investment and funding.

Investment and Funding

The successful development of AI-related products, including expert systems to run on mainframes and smaller computers, necessarily depends upon adequate funding. In fact there are several sources of funds available to new ('start-up') companies in the expert systems sector. Johnson (1984) has cited, as sources of funds:

— advance payments and sales;

— venture capital and public offerings;

— public research funds.

The importance of venture capital for the development of commercial applications is emphasised. As we may expect, the venture capital scene in the UK is less active than elsewhere. AI Ltd is an example of a company that has raised capital to operate in Britain: this firm now has the franchise to market the Xerox 1108 in the UK. Examples of venture capital funding for start-up companies in the US are shown in Table 1.3

The route to profitability, following a company start-up, is not an easy one. There are relatively few genuine AI specialists available and, despite the highly optimistic market projections, it is still true that individual projects remain speculative. None of the companies shown in Table 1.3 has yet achieved an unambiguous commercial viability. There is often a heavy dependence on a small number of skilled staff, a circumstance that adds little to company security.

Venture capital has traditionally favoured investment in the development of hardware, though this seems less relevant in the field of expert systems. It seems inevitable that the major computer manufacturers will develop their own AI-related products, and that the market could well be dominated by standard hardware. And it is likely that the role of the systems house could grow in a commercial expert-systems environment, strengthening the role of the systems house relative to the hardware manufacturers.

Government funding will continue as a vital source of investment in the emerging AI industry. We have already glanced at the role of Alvey, DARPA, Esprit, etc (funds from these sources are shown in Table 1.4).

Start-up Company	Amount Committed	Sources
SOFTWARE COMPANIES		
Dynaquest	$1 million	R & D limited parternship, 33 investors
Inference Corp	$3 million	Venrock, Merrill Lynch and others
IntelliCorp	$2 million $10 million	Chargeurs Public offering
Teknowledge	$7 million $10 to $15 million	Industrial companies and banks 1984 figure
Thinking Machine	$5 million	J H Whitney & Co, private investors
HARDWARE COMPANIES		
Lisp Machine Inc	$5.5 million	13 institutional investors
Symbolics	$30 million	General Electric, General Instruments, Harvard Trust, Bank of Boston, etc

Table 1.3   Venture Capital Funding of AI Start-up Companies
(Source: Johnson, 1984)

Country	Project	Period	Total Funding	AI Projects	Sources of Funds
USA	DARPA Strategic Computing	1984-8	$600 million	$100 million	Government 100%
UK	Alvey Programme	1984-8	$525 million	$49 million	Government 57% industry 43%
EEC	Esprit	1984-8	$1330 million	$90 million	Government 50% industry 50%
Japan	Fifth-generation	1983-5	$30 million	$30 million	Government 100%

Table 1.4   Government Funding of AI-related Projects
(Source: Johnson, 1984)

It is obvious that substantial funds, from various sources, are already being made available for the development of expert systems. One estimate (Johnson, 1984) is that during 1984 $90 million in the US and $9 million in the UK were invested for this purpose. Japan is spending a similar amount to the UK, and there are many parallel projects that will aid the development of commercial expert systems. However, as yet only a small proportion of the investment is being recouped from expert systems sold in the marketplace.

The availability of finance for the development of expert systems and other AI-related products will depend upon assessments of likely return (a conventional enough investment criterion). However, the position is confused in the case of AI because there is too little understanding of its current nature and future potential. The AI buff in a university or company laboratory may or may not be able to define expert systems in ways that have commercial significance, but unless venture capitalists, senior managers, government ministers and others have a clear concept of the economic potential of AI-related products then investment, from whatever source, is likely to be both inadequate in volume and misdirected. This is one of the topics relevant to financing discussed by William Janeway, vice-president and director of the US investment banking firm, F Ederstadt and Company (in Winston and Prendergast, eds, 1984).

In some circumstances investment may occur where there is little concept of what it will yield, where there is no shared agreement about the nature of the activity being funded. Janeway cites a venture financed in the London capital market at the time of the South Sea Bubble: this venture was one 'whose purpose will be disclosed at a later time'. We may expect modern venture capitalists to be less than satisfied with such an ill-defined enterprise.

Efforts to define the scope of artificial intelligence are bedevilled by the emotive character of much of the AI-linked language. Venture capital and government interest may be discouraged by what is perceived as a hair-brained or frivolous terminology. It has been said that when philosophy yields truths it is no longer philosophy but logic, science or some such. Janeway makes a nice point when he observes, in the same spirit, that 'Artificial Intelligence ceases to be Artificial Intelligence when it enters the real world, at which point it becomes something like advanced Computer Science'. The corollary is that real progress in AI can be represented as incremental advances in computer science, an interpretation that AI-naive venture capitalists might find reassuring.

In any event there will be efforts to subject AI developments to the discipline of finance. If, in the short term, individuals with access to capital are seduced by fashionable hype then the test will come at the time when the funding is expected to deliver marketable products. The necessary estimates of likely return will prevent long-term investment on a vicarious basis. Those who allocate funds will expect results – which is why AI specialists and others are worried about the current 'overselling' of expert and related systems. The AI fraternity is eventually succeeding – at least partly for a variety of military and strategic reasons – in attracting investment from various sources. It remains to be seen whether the AI industry will deliver in the ways the investors require.

EXPERT AND OTHER SYSTEMS

General

We have already seen, in discussing mindware and related products, that there is a growing family of software systems that attempt to reflect mental or psychological phenomena. Many of these products are on the fringes of AI: they may be expected to benefit from progress in artificial intelligence but in general do not at present rely on the heuristic and other processes that define AI proper. Elsewhere there are other systems that relate, in one way or another, to AI software but which do not necessarily exhibit specific AI features. In this context it is worth drawing attention to *decision support systems, advisory systems, interactive information systems* and related facilities. It is obvious that expert systems can aid decision making, provide advice and allow interactive working – as can a wide range of software that cannot claim an expert-systems status. Again what emerges is a relatively loose vocabulary that creates the illusion of precision. We can explore, for example, *decision support systems* to highlight typical categorisations.

Decision Support Systems

Decision support systems (DSS) are sometimes defined in ways that would serve equally for expert systems. Thus Coleman (1984) defines a decision support system as 'a set of integrated software, designed to assist in the managerial function of decision-making'. Many business-oriented expert systems (see Chapter 3) are designed to aid decision making in such a fashion. Freyenfeld (1984), recognising the terminological confusion in the field and required to produce a definition of decision support systems, offered a version 'generally accepted as valid and useful by representatives of some 30 supplier, user, and academic organisations in the UK':

> 'A DECISION SUPPORT SYSTEM is an *interactive* data processing and display system which is used to *assist* in a *concurrent* decision-making process, and which also conforms to the following characteristics:
>
> *i* it is sufficiently *user-friendly* to be used by the decision maker(s) *in person*.
>
> *ii* it displays its information in a *format* and *terminology* which is familiar to its user(s).
>
> *iii* it is *selective* in its provision of information and *avoids* exposing its user(s) to an *information overload*.'.

As with most expert systems, it is reckoned that decision support systems can *assist* decision making rather than usurp the proper human role. At the same time, it is undeniable that some expert systems can outperform most human beings in the same area. DSS, as the name implies, are generally required to leave scope for human thought and judgement.

Again, as we find with many expert systems, the DSS package is actually a tool which enables a purchaser to construct a dedicated facility for particular purposes. This task may require computer expertise in the purchasing company, though it may be relatively easy to set up certain systems of a particular type. Freyenfeld (1984) identifies six distinct types of decision support systems:

— chief executive information systems;

— commercial operational analysis and planning systems;

— industrial operational analysis and planning systems;

— preference determination systems;

— cognitive mapping systems;

— expert advisory systems.

In several of these categories there are systems that would be affected by developments in artificial intelligence, but *expert advisory systems* is the category most relevant to the theme of the present book. Here lie the software products, available for mainframes and smaller machines, that are deemed to incorporate AI features in order to fulfil an advisory or counselling role. Hence expert systems, in some versions offering decision support, allow the user to enter into an interactive dialogue during which the system can offer advice, proffer decisions and also explain the reasoning that yields the conclusions.

The future is likely to see expert systems working in conjunction with other types of decision support software to aid business activity in many different areas. In such a way, integrated software will come to address many of the planning and financial decisions that occur at the various levels of a company. Freyenfeld draws attention to Tymshare's REVEAL as the first system in the UK market to combine the features of an expert system shell and an operational analysis and planning system generator. The system has facilities for graphics, modelling, analysis, report generation and data management. As befits an AI-related product there is also scope for handling uncertain ('fuzzy') data and for reasoning in various modes.

Operational research techniques and expert systems facilities are also combined in a Route Planning Aid developed for the US Air Force by Systems Control Technology, SCICON's US subsidiary. And a system called MATADOR (MATerials ADvice ORganiser), to be used in the Household Consumables Division which manufactures and markets throughout the world, will comprise five modules:

— an expert health & safety assurance system;

— an ingredients' suppliers database and data dictionary;

— a product formulation advisor, using dynamic programming;

— a marketing-oriented expert system advising on
  consumer-perceived attributes;

— an interactive front-end.

MATADOR is seen as one of several systems that combines
expert systems with other forms of decision support. Various companies, including ICI and BL's Istel, are working along similar
lines. Hence another mode of convergence is evident. It is interesting to reflect how the many systems and techniques subsumed
under the proliferating buzz-word categories – *expert systems,
decision support systems, mindware, integrated software,* etc –
variously merge, converge, overlap and coalesce.

The REVEAL package (cited by Freyenfeld and discussed, for
example, by Warren, 1984) can be represented as a decision-
support program that exploits AI techniques. Produced by Tymshare's subsidiary, InfoTym Corporation, it is intended – according
to David Morley, director of sales and marketing – to put the facts
together 'so that a human mind can decide the direction'. Jack
Greer, a business consultant on expert systems for InfoTym, has
remarked that REVEAL is 'a bicycle, not a jet plane' – 'it lets the
user cut things down into manageable tasks'. The product can be
regarded as a 'mind spreadsheet' that uses various inference
abilities to classify information and to assist in decision making.

The various REVEAL features – database-management system, graphics, report generator, etc – can be exploited on mainframes and smaller systems. Thus the system can be used on an
IBM 370 mainframe, a DEC VAX minicomputer, and an IBM
PC/XT. A special facility allows information to be transferred
('ported') from a mainframe to a mini or micro and back again,
with the central aim of creating a complete software environment.
The package is flexible enough to exploit dedicated knowledge
bases for almost any business function. (At early-1985 prices, the
REVEAL product is priced at $50,000 for mainframes, and
$25,000 for minicomputers. The price for the PC version varies.

For users who have a mainframe licence the price is $2,000; and for others, a minimum of ten PC licences can be purchased for $4,000 each. It is expected that the necessary knowledge templates will cost between $500 and $2,000 each, depending upon the level of expertise and the subject matter.)

Other decision support systems may have various integrated facilities but may not exploit AI techniques. For example, the FISCAL package from Microdata incorporates financial modelling, database management, reporting, graphics, forecasting and econometrics, but does not claim conventional expert systems features. Use is made of an English-like syntax to aid effective interactive working, and many 'what-if?' options can be explored through simple commands. FISCAL is intended as a financial planning system for top management, accountants, planners and analysts. Many other companies – for example, ICL, IBM, Comshare, etc (see Mill, 1984) – are developing decision support systems for various purposes.

A Californian start-up company is marketing a package called Lightyear – named after the firm – able to rank a number of alternatives to a solution according to criteria entered by the executive (see Bartimo, 1984). A user can go backwards through the program to re-evaluate the criteria or to compare a final evaluation with a different one achieved by another user of Lightyear (Bartimo: 'it aids the executive in shaping a decision – not in making it, as so-called expert systems do'). The system provides an effective organisation of ideas: Lightyear belongs to the class of ideas processors that we have already met (see above). This is one package in a proliferating family that aid decision making on the fringes of artificial intelligence.

Efforts have been made to indicate the main features of decision support systems. Jones (1984), for example, draws attention to characteristics of the best decision support tools: we note the requirement for information held within the organisation, the need to analyse such information in an unstructured way, the requirement for facilities for calculation and modelling, the need to exploit the latest software and hardware developments. Perhaps most interestingly, we find hints at the future direction of decision support systems, an evolution that will be greatly affected by progress in artificial intelligence. The development of increasingly effective expert systems will necessarily influence the DSS scene. Current decision support facilities that embody no AI provisions are likely to be supplanted as expert systems become more adept. We may see DSS and expert systems evolving in parallel with evident convergence in some areas. But it is hard to envisage a prolonged evolution of non-AI DSS when it becomes increasingly easy to incorporate effective expert systems provisions into economic decision-aiding (–making?) software.

THE MICRO IMPACT

One of the most far-reaching developments in the computer industry was the invention of the microprocessor about fifteen years ago. In a few years this has led to the emergence of thousands of micro-based products, a vast array of commercial systems that were to influence all areas of human activity. Microprocessors, serving as the central processing units (CPUs) of a new family of computing units, microcomputers, made it possible to extend computer power into many unprecedented areas. Throughout the 1970s it became possible to obtain cheap computer power for countless purposes. By the 1980s the microcomputer, by virtue of several converging technologies, was able to take on a range of computer applications formerly the province of the expensive mainframe (see Chapter 2). The likely impact of the micro in the years ahead has not yet been fully considered.

There is debate as to the extent to which microcomputers can cope with certain types of formerly mainframe-oriented tasks. With AI and related techniques the debate is compounded and intensified. Artificial intelligence is itself controversial enough, as is the discernible migration of applications from mainframes to micros. Add one controversy to another and the debate becomes doubly fraught.

As with most controversies the AI/micro debate has its poles. Thus Watt (1984) can declare that 'the truth of the matter, however, is that real artificial intelligence is not yet available on microcomputers', though able to remark in the same article that in the past few years, as micros have become more powerful and capable, 'they have been taken seriously as vehicles for AI applications'. Moreover it is pointed out that Lisp, a key language for artificial intelligence, is moving onto microcomputers. As one example, Gold Hill Computers of Cambridge, Massachusetts, has recently introduced Golden Common Lisp, which adapts Common Lisp (funded by DARPA for AI purposes) for micro-based personal computers. And an increasing range of AI-related products are being made available for microcomputers (see Chapter 5). Tony Durham (1984) emphasises that 'expert systems, speech, vision kits, and other manifestations of AI are all becoming available for microcomputers'.

The growing availability of AI-related products for micros is paralleled by the emergence of, for example, decision support systems able to run on small systems. Some manufacturers of DSS are being encouraged to write micro versions of their mainframe software to operate on personal computers. Here the cut-down versions may depend upon the increasingly prevalent micro/mainframe links so that there is still access to the mainframe capabilities of a host computer (for data, not processing power). An alternative is to use a more powerful microcomputer (eg a Motorola 68000-based multiuser machine) to run a full version of the software. In short, make the software easier to handle or use a more powerful micro.

The newly emerging accessibility and user-friendliness of micro-based decision support and expert systems is enabling small companies to acquire sophisticated software where formerly price would have been prohibitive. It has been pointed out that a new demand for software has been created by the spread of microcomputers and computer literacy. One consequence has been the impact on companies that already operate mainframe systems. Users may have limited access to a mainframe, a circumstance that can encourage an exploration of alternative micro-based options. A 32-bit 'supermicro', for example, can handle a wide range of sophisticated software, yet is relatively cheap and can sit on a desk. There can be little doubt that the micro impact will grow in the years to come.

BEYOND FIFTH GENERATION

There are plenty of signs that imaginative computer researchers

are looking to the sorts of technologies that will follow the realisation of fifth-generation computers in the 1990s. Speaking at a
recent SRI international conference on advanced information
technology, Professor Hideo Aiso, of the Japanese research organisation ICOT, commented: 'There is a design group planning to set
up a sixth-generation computer systems project. The main
research target is the analysis of the human brain, application of
biochemistry and development of biological chips; study of optical
computing; analysis of communications processes, psychological
effects and so on'. It is thought that the project will be under way in
about two years.

In this connection we may see, for example, revolutionary
man/machine interface techniques – including direct brain/
computer links. Already some military aircraft have sensors to
respond to pilot eye movements, and there is talk of systems that
will read brainwaves to control air disposition, weapons, etc. Elec-
trodes placed on the user's neck and head may be employed, as
with modern lie detectors, to pick up and interpret significant
signals. In sixth-generation systems, one option would be to
replace today's sensors by effective protein-based biochips, now
being developed. The provision of three-dimensional protein
lattices will have, as one consequence, a capacity for denser information packing and ever smaller units for data processing. In such
circumstances it will be possible for a wide range of microcomputers to handle immensely sophisticated software. The AI/micro
debate will be of historical academic interest and nothing more.

SUMMARY

This chapter has outlined some of the main factors that are
influencing the development of AI and expert systems and related
products in the mid-1980s, with specific reference to the
emergence of such systems for microcomputers. Some elements of
the AI controversy have been highlighted and some thoughts
provided on the current scale of the AI impact. It is significant, for
example, that after decades of lethargy towards AI, governments
throughout the developed world are realising the importance of
investment in the related and overlapping fields of artificial intelligence, expert systems and fifth-generation computers.

An attempt has been made to indicate some parallel software developments – for example, in 'mindware' and decision support systems – which, though often on the fringes of artificial intelligence, operate in the intellectual, psychological or interactive fields where we will increasingly find AI-based products and techniques. We have also drawn attention to prevailing vocabularies, indicating that they can be variously emotive, imprecise and confusing. Investment and funding policies are at least partly influenced by *images* of possible products, and there is concern that extravagant vocabularies, leading to an overselling of AI-related systems, may cause funds to evaporate – as has happened at other moments in the history of computer technology (for example, in the funding of automatic language-translation systems). Some details of the current investment and funding situation have been included.

This introductory chapter, providing information and speculation about the present computer-technology scene (and brief speculation about the future), has given a framework against which specific aspects of expert systems and microcomputers can be considered in later chapters. In this area, as elsewhere, we are conscious of converging and interacting trends and developments. It is important to bear this in mind while trying to appreciate the dynamics of a rapidly evolving technology.

2 The Microcomputer Advance

INTRODUCTION

There have been many key trends in the development of the computer industry. We need only recall, for example, the emergence of new electronic technologies in the progress from one computer generation to the next, the gradual proliferation of high-level languages for specific application purposes, and the expansion of computer competence into one commercial or industrial field after another. One important and continuing trend, initiated in the early-1970s, is the growing impact of computer systems based on microprocessors. For the first time it became possible to achieve programmable computation in cheap and miniscule systems. This allowed computer systems to be usefully embedded in a wide range of other products, and also brought computer power within the reach of a much greater spectrum of users.

For more than a decade the scope and power of micro-based systems have progressively increased. This chapter gives the background to the micro advance, highlights important aspects of the current scene, indicates how micros are growing in power and intelligence, and gives a few pointers to the future. There are already a number of commercial expert systems available for microcomputers (see Chapter 5). Critics may argue that such products do not contain 'true AI', but when the software possibilities are considered against the framework of growing micro competence, the manufacturers' claims about micro-based expert systems do not seem extravagant. Already microcomputers can cope with a range of applications that would, a decade ago, have

seemed unthinkable. Expert systems are now working, with varying degrees of effectiveness, in a wide variety of industrial, commercial and scientific environments. We should not be too surprised if a migration of software from mainframes to smaller
systems occurs here, as is occurring in other applications areas.

THE MICRO BACKGROUND

The idea of a programmable computer is normally traced to the
nineteenth century (Charles Babbage and Ada Lovelace), though
many concepts relevant to computing were explored before that
time. The basic design (or architecture) for a programmable computer was first realised electronically in the 1940s: various *electrical*, as opposed to *electronic*, systems were built in the 1930s but do
not seem to have much of a profile in the history of the computer
industry.

The early glass-valve computers (eg ENIAC in 1946) were
supplanted by transistor-based models in the 1950s and 1960s.
When William Shockley, John Bardeen and Walter Brattain first
demonstrated the transistor in 1948 in the Bell Telephone
Laboratories, they were laying the basis for the solid-state technology that would yield the microprocessor in the early 1970s. The
first micro, produced by the Intel Corporation in 1971, was based
on a single $\frac{1}{4}$-in-square silicon chip which carried the equivalent of
2250 transistors, all the necessary CPU circuitry for a tiny computer. By 1976, chips of this size could carry more than 20,000
electronic components, and today there is talk of building chips
with up to a million circuit elements.

Current microprocessors, densely packaged with electronic
components, serve in thousands of applications – embedded in
cars, aircraft, missiles, domestic appliances, communications networks, industrial robots, scientific instrumentation, toys, etc; or
serving as the CPUs in computers ranging from the cheap home
systems to 'supermicros' and minicomputers costing tens of
thousands of pounds. As micros evolve ever more complex component architectures they are able to handle increasingly sophisticated software. The first micros were usually confined to simple
control functions (for example, supervising operations in petrol
pumps) whereas today they are flexing their muscles with database

systems, decision support facilities, and expert systems. The remarkable evolution of the micro in only fifteen years has proved to be one of the most dramatic subplots in the story of the computer industry.

Part of the background to the modern micro is the convergence of various technological trends, evident in other contexts but influential here also. For example, the increased use of teletext and viewdata in the UK has not occurred in isolation from developments in microcomputers. National teletext campaigns were carried out in 1981 and 1982 which, by the end of 1982, boosted teletext sets to 700,000. Today there are more than two million teletext sets in use in the UK, and one estimate (cited by Pattie, 1985) suggested that 98% of the world's viewdata/teletext sets installed in seventeen countries make use of sets made in Britain. At the same time, microcomputers designed to display viewdata pages in full colour are becoming increasingly available, exploiting progress in higher-level graphics (such as photovideotex and DRCS, dynamically redefinable character sets). This is a clear instance of convergence in information technology.

Much has been written about the spread of microcomputers in schools in the UK and elsewhere (we may judge it ultimate benediction or kiss-of-death, according to taste, that the House of Lords chose to discuss school micros as a key issue in their first televised debate on 23rd January 1985). Today more than 10% of British homes have a home computer, a higher proportion than in the US. This circumstance, occasioned by the efforts of such firms as Sinclair and Acorn, will have far-reaching implications when truly intelligent software becomes widely available to micro owners. Already we can see how the proliferation of microcomputers has stimulated the efforts of software suppliers to exploit this commercial sector.

At the same time it is easy to find notes of caution sounded on the micro scene. Here too, as with expert systems, there is hype and overselling; and debate on the real scope of micro-based facilities. It may be fashionable, for example, for companies to acquire personal microcomputers for managers and other staff. But are such computers always used properly? Djurdjevic (1984) asks 'is the PC mania merely a fad?'. For instance, the *Fortune* 1000 companies were expected to purchase more than 700,000 personal computers in 1984. But, it is asked, how effectively are all these computers being used? Djurdjevic: 'I asked that question of a number of client executives who either personally owned a PC, or had access to one at work. Most of them sheepishly admitted to have personally benefited very little from their micro'. The suggestion is that micro-linked technologies often run ahead of users' abilities to assimilate them. This is clearly true of microcomputers acquired prematurely by companies (in the absence of appropriate training for potential users) for conventional business applications. It will also be true, in the absence of adequate user preparation, when AI-related functions become widely available on microcomputers.

INTERNATIONAL TRENDS

General

The international micro scene is one of increasing microcomputer power in a situation of growing market pressures on established companies and new start-up enterprises. A prodigious growth in all sectors of the micro market has now (in 1985) slowed considerably and a predicted shake-out – signalled by bankruptcies, plummeting financial returns, and strategic price cuts for hardware and other products – is now under way (see Micros in Competition, below). A recent (late-1984) National Computing Centre (NCC)/ *Computing* survey of the UK business micro market finds a variety of fluctuations in the various micro sectors of the national computer industry. For example, according to the NCC database, 90 systems have been withdrawn from the market, with around 80 having been added. In software, IBM compatibility is increasingly popular, and a large number of older packages have been withdrawn. Until December a steady growth in all the micro sectors – hardware, training, software and support – was evident. However there are signs that the trend has now changed. Growth has slowed and many companies are in trouble. At the same time, micro competence, albeit in a constantly fluctuating product base, continues to develop.

The market fluctuations evident in the UK have their counterparts in Europe and elsewhere, albeit with local peculiarities.

France, for example, with a National Electronics Plan (or Filiere Electronique), has made considerable progress – both by means of indigenous effort and by effective transfer of US technology. But it is still recognised that France lacks the sort of lively domestic market for microcomputers that can be found in Britain. Brigitte Morel of Intelligent Electronics, a leading Paris-based market research organisation for the European microcomputer industry, has observed that the French 'have caught on late in this area and they are a long way from becoming a serious manufacturing contender' (quoted by Gee, 1985).

There are still hopes, on the part of the Mitterand government (which faces a general election in 1986), that the French nation will become more conscious of information technology. President Mitterand has asked Gilbert Trigano, founder of the Club Mediterranee holiday village empire, to supervise a scheme to install computer workshops in towns and villages. It is expected that companies with manufacturing plants in France will receive privileged treatment in the workshops – so companies such as Sinclair and Apple are said to be contemplating manufacturing their products in France. We may expect the return of a conservative government in 1986, if it occurs, to have consequences for the Filiere Electronique and moves to spread micros through the French population.

Elsewhere in Europe a similar growth in personal computing is predicted. Recent joint research (involving the journal *Computerworld*, Intelligent Electronics and International Data Corporation) showed that the personal computer market in the Netherlands is expected to grow by no less than 50%/year over the coming years (Blakeney, 1984/85: the Netherlands 'is devouring low-end technology faster than any other'). This trend is expected to result in an installed user base of 250,000 micro units by 1989. Similarly, in Spain a market growth of 50% is expected this year (1985).

In the Soviet Union also there are dramatic plans to increase the number of microprocessor-based products. Thus over the first three years of the 1981-1985 five-year plan the production of microprocessors increased almost five-fold and the manufacture of microcomputers almost doubled. Facilities are being enlarged in the mini-machines (MM) batch, which includes advanced mini and microcomputers designed for many different purposes.

A wide range of microcomputers is produced in the Soviet Union though some of the models bear a striking resemblance to earlier Western machines. Many computer complexes are configured on the basis of Elektronica-60 microcomputers for control functions, dialogue computer complexes (personal computers), and home computers. There are current plans to produce a wide and expanding spectrum of software – standard programs, program-generation systems, automatic debugging sets, etc – for various classes of computers, including microcomputers. The State Fund of Algorithms and Programs promotes the wide use of standard programs, currently numbering almost 30,000. Many Soviet schemes are developed in conjunction with other countries via the Intergovernmental Commission for Co-operation in Computer Engineering of the Socialist Countries, involving organisations from Cuba, Eastern Europe and the Soviet Union.

Compared with the West, the socialist bloc has been slow to develop the potential of personal computers and many other micro-based systems. Alex Tatarinov, who worked as a programmer in the USSR, has been quoted (by Needle and Besher, 1984): 'There were no personal computers at all in Russia when I was there three years ago'. In September 1984, the Soviet Union announced the launch of a fifteen-year program to teach students to use Soviet-made personal computers called AGATs. One of these desktop systems, produced by ELORG (Electronorgteknika), was shown as a prototype at a Moscow trade fair in July 1983. The AGAT is seen by at least one Western observer (Bores, 1984) as a bad copy of the Apple II ('The operating system and ROM seemed to be a direct lift . . .'), and it is pointed out that Soviet copying of Western products is not unprecedented: copies of IBM 1401s and 370s are currently in use in Russia.

The AGAT computer is slowly being introduced into Soviet schools but this is unlikely to herald an explosion of personal-computer interest among Soviet citizens – or perhaps even among professionals who may be expected to benefit from economic computer facilities. David Ditlya, who worked as a mechanical engineer in Kishinev, has observed: 'There were no personal computers when I was there. Maybe they have micros now, but I had friends who were high-level managers and programmers and they didn't use micros. They all used big computers' (quoted by Needle and Besher).

The current Soviet plan requires that 1131 AGATs be delivered to Soviet schools in 1985, a modest aim by Western standards. It is suggested that by the year 2000, one million Soviet students each year will be taught how to use computers: again a highly conservative scheme compared with what is already happening in the UK, the US and other Western countries. At the same time, with a different cultural and economic base to the US, the Soviet Union may have less requirement for micros. Charles Lecht, a high-technology consultant who has testified before US congressional committees, has observed that when the Soviets need micros they will make them. There are already Russian plans for research and development in fifth-generation systems (see, for example, Walton and Tate, 1984), and activities in this area may be expected to have implications for microcomputers and other micro-based systems.

Japan also intends, with growing commitment, to attack the low end of the computer market. The aim is to sell the MSX standard operating system micros on a worldwide basis. Already Canon, Hitachi, JVC, Mitsubishi, Sanyo, Sony and Toshiba have all manufactured micros to the MSX specification devised by Microsoft, a US software company. The compatibility of the Japanese MSX systems is regarded as an important selling feature, though it is also pointed out that MSX technology is too old fashioned to be successful in a sophisticated marketplace.

Elsewhere in Asia there is already a prodigious and growing involvement in the international computer industry. Many semi-conductor multinationals rely on plants in South-East Asia for chip production, and national aspirations increasingly focus on hi-tech developments (see, for example, Burstein, 1984, for discussion of computer trends and attitudes in Singapore). A worldwide computer culture is evolving with consequences for microcomputer usage in industry, commerce and other environments. The massive base of potential micro users throughout the world is now provoking intense competition between manufacturers and suppliers of microcomputers and related products.

MICROS IN COMPETITION

Nineteen eighty-four has been depicted as the year in which microcomputer supply finally met demand, a circumstance that dubbed 1985 as the 'micro shake-out year'. This in fact is a complex scenario. We may scrutinise micro demand on a national basis or internationally (embracing both the developed world and the Third World). Demand is a flexible phenomenon, mediated by purchasing power and political exigency as much as by psychological inclination. But this said, there is little doubt that by the end of 1985 the shape of the international microcomputer industry will have changed considerably.

There are today about 350 companies throughout the world producing microcomputers. This year, it is predicted, many of these firms will fall by the wayside and the market turmoil will persist for some time. One observer (Kenneth Lim, an analyst with Dataquest, quoted by Sullivan, 1984/85) suggests that by the end of 1986 only 75 firms will remain in the field, with more than half the number – between 40 and 45 companies – residing in the US.

Today analysts agree that the market is too crowded. New start-up companies have been attracted by the remarkable growth in microcomputer sales revenues in the 1980s – gains of 130% in 1983 over 1982, and 85% in 1984 over 1983 – but the gain for 1985 over 1984 is set at around 35%. Lim: 'Most companies don't have a chance. They don't have the resources to match up with the major players in the industry. They don't have the money for advertising, marketing, distributing, establishing dealer networks or penetrating niche markets'. One of the main factors that firms have to contend with is the impact of IBM.

Most observers agree that IBM will become more dominant in the personal-computer market throughout 1985, though there is also the suggestion (for example, in Blakeney, 1984/85) that IBM's market penetration in 1984 fell short of 'the vendor's own great expectations' – the IBM PCjr is not expected to appear in many countries. During 1983 IBM's share of the world micro market, in the business and professional sector, hovered slightly about 25%, followed by Apple, Tandy, Osborne, etc. There is discernible feeling in Europe that IBM will eventually dominate. (Research by Intelligent Electronics suggests that users are highly satisfied with IBM personal computers and with IBM as a company.)

Various factors have been taken as signalling IBM's strength in the personal-computer sector – recent price reductions, the introduction of the Personal Computer PC/AT, the Topview operating environment, and the business software series. One suggestion is that IBM will change direction when the market levels out: the firm may move away from MS-DOS and Xenix, and establish a proprietary operating system for its personal-computer range. Firms boasting MS-DOS compatibility would hardly welcome such a move.

Apple Computer Inc, which has avoided IBM compatibility, may have enhanced survival chances thereby, supporting a large group of system users who are not into IBM. Other companies, favouring compatibility, may be less fortunate as IBM changes tack. AT & T, for example, has been depicted as too locked into PC-DOS. But companies may survive by focusing on a market niche and by not being unrealistically ambitious.

The IBM micro price cuts in 1984 were paralleled by price-reduction announcements by other companies in 1984 and early-1985. In June 1984 IBM cut personal-computer prices by up to 23%. As a typical example, a Personal Computer with 256K bytes of random-access memory and dual floppy drives (but no monitor) was repriced from $2908 to $2420 (cited by Bender, 1984/85). Later in the year there were further price adjustments, and competition between IBM's PCjr and Apple Computer's Apple IIe and IIc system put further pressure on price levels. By the end of 1984 some US retailers were offering a 256K byte, dual-floppy Personal Computer (with monitor) for less than $2000.

In the summer (1984) other manufacturers followed IBM with price reductions. This was particularly noticeable among PC-compatible suppliers, but others – including DEC – also followed suit. The Apple Macintosh saw a price cut in September from $2495 to $2195, with retail prices now (1985) well below $2000. Already there is speculation about more price cuts to come, and one observer (George Colony of Forrester Research in Cambridge, Mass) has predicted a 'fire sale'.

Price changes have also occurred at the low end of the micro-computer market. In the UK, Acorn saw its market share dropping in early-1985, and the company's main rival, Sinclair Research, dropped the price of the Spectrum Plus by £50 to a new recommended retail price of £129.95, at the same time increasing production to 200,000 computers a month. Sir Clive Sinclair was quoted in January 1985 as expecting the home computer market to enter a 'very vigorous phase' ('we anticipate strong competition from US manufacturers in particular'). The home computer market is likely to settle at lower levels, with foreign competition growing at the same time. This is one reason why both Acorn and Sinclair are working to move up market.

In February 1985, Oric, the Ascot-based home computer company which claims to supply more than 50% of the French home-computer market, was placed in the hands of the receiver. At that time the company had £3 million unsold stock of its £100-200 machines. At the same time, Acorn was calling off six-month merger talks with Torch Computers. Here a key factor was thought to be Acorn's collapsed share price and low stock market standing. Torch commented that the split was because of a 'divergence of plans about the future'. On February 6th, 1985, Acorn asked for its shares to be temporarily suspended, and on February 20th it was announced that Olivetti had taken a 49.3% stake in the company with a majority-stake option.

Commodore, in contrast to other micro suppliers, announced in February that it had no plans to reduce the price of any of its products. And the new company Amstrad also declared an intention to maintain its current price structure. Commodore, however, has announced staff cuts (114 at Corby) to meet the diminished market expectations. This may be compared, albeit favourably, with the Oric reduction in personnel – from about 100 to 37 – before the receiver was called in. And Prism, once the foremost distributor of Sinclair products, also collapsed in early-1985. David Broad, director of the British Micro-Computer Manufacturers Association, was quoted: 'This is turning into a bad week for the industry, and not one that augurs well for 1985 . . .'.

Apart from revamping the price structures or cutting staff numbers, microcomputer manufacturers can take various actions to survive through 1985 and beyond. Sullivan (1984/85) notes various guidelines suggested by analysts:

— jump ahead in terms of technology;

— find market niches (be content with 0.01% market share);

— grow big enough to maintain independence. Spend up to $20 million on advertising, and a similar amount on R & D. Develop a strong dealer base;

— watch the corporate financial health;

— reduce production costs by designing low-cost, efficient manufacturing plants. Consider moving offshore;

— end eternal production development cycles;

— sell aggressively;

— establish a corporate framework that allows a good solid management team to be brought in as the company grows.

We may speculate on what such plays will do for the microcomputer market in the years ahead. In broad terms it seems likely that we will see fewer companies in the field, but with dramatically enhanced product offerings. Such a scenario will have profound effects on the micro application spectrum, not least on the capacity of micros to handle expert systems and other AI-related software. It is worth looking at how the scope for microcomputers is already being enlarged.

ENLARGING SCOPE FOR MICROS

General

We have noted the jostling of many microcomputers in the marketplace. Companies variously face commercial difficulties or secure a viable market share. In January 1985, for example, it was announced that Olivetti was to launch an IBM PC/AT compatible micro as part of an effort to become Europe's top supplier of personal computers (see report in *Computer News*, 24/1/85, p 4). The Olivetti personal computer division aims to generate one third of the company's UK revenues. Paul Mahoney, ex-head of the large systems division and brought in to run the new campaign, has said: 'The company is looking at PCs as being the most important product over the next couple of years – it is the workstation of the future'. Initially the focus will be on the key product, the M24 micro, and also on the M21 and M10 machines. In addition to the new hardware offerings (see also Technology, below), there are other signs that the scope for micros is rapidly expanding.

The Economist Intelligence Unit (EIU) has recently (in late-1984) predicted a six-fold expansion of the UK microcomputer software market over the next few years. It is also suggested (eg by Arthur, 1984) that even conservative estimates predict a tripling of the market. The EIU report, 'The European Markets for Microcomputer Software', based on interviews with top managers and a survey of micro companies, forecasts a 40% annual growth in real terms from the 1983 revenue of £127 million to a figure for 1988 of £750 million. Increases are expected in the market shares of integrated packages, home software, mainframe/micro links and educational software, with declines predicted for stand-alone packages, arcade games and languages.

Another trend is towards running applications designed originally for mainframes on smaller systems. For example, Fedanzo (1984) discusses this possibility in connection with running Cobol applications on microcomputers. With 'relatively minor modifications' it is possible to transport many existing mainframe and minicomputer applications to 16-bit micros, a move that is encouraged by the cost of creating replacement application systems and the backlog of systems development in many companies.

It is also possible to treat Fortran applications in a similar way. Fortran 77 code can be transported from, say, an HP 3000 minicomputer to an IBM Personal Computer or an HP 150, after only a few I/O syntax changes. Similarly, scientific Fortran applications can, following simple modifications to the source, be moved from one system to another.

The obvious advantage to business, scientific and other users is that quite sophisticated applications can be implemented on relatively cheap machines. For instance, micro-based distributed data processing (DDP) can be implemented on a 256K byte system with two floppy disk drives. Such a configuration can be used to convert 2000-line Cobol programs that access files containing thousands of records. Micros can be used as workbenches for programmers dealing with Cobol, but since micros are stand-alone systems in their own right they can be employed to handle a growing range of normal Cobol and Fortran tasks. The programming environment now available on 16-bit micros has been compared to that available on minis and mainframes during the 1970s. It is possible to implement Cobol and Fortran applications on microcomputers but allowed project times should take into account the fact that the fast development tools available for the larger systems are not yet on the market for micros.

The scope for micros is being enlarged by means of various design and expansion ploys. For instance, one approach that exploits the microcomputer's hardware flexibility can reduce the number of support chips and achieve enhanced operational efficiency (see McCracken, 1984). Similarly using add-on components, the scope of a micro-based facility can be dramatically enlarged. Winchester disks, for example, can be added to the BBC Microcomputer to achieve a powerful business machine. And there are reasons for believing that the gradual evolution of micro potential will progressively erode the mainframe position. Thus Healey (1983) portrays a scene of 'the relatively gentle demise of the mainframe with a gradual takeover of the micro'. In this view, we will see the complete demise of the mainframe within ten years. A number of factors are contributing to this dramatic development:

— progress in large-scale integration (LSI) technology. Two years ago a 256K byte memory needed 128 chips, whereas today the count is down to eight;

— progress in software technology (caused by LSI progress). It is suggested that current editors and compilers on micros are ahead of those on mainframes;

— extended addressing capability on micros. Microcomputers can now catch up with systems like the IBM System/34. Micro CPUs with the power of small mainframes will be available within two years;

— increased storage for micros. With Winchester technology, disks are available that can hold up to 20M bytes. By 1985, $5\frac{1}{4}$-inch Winchester drives will have 500M byte capacities, so eroding a traditional mainframe advantage;

— increased availability of networks (eg LANs), allowing

effective distributed processing on a local basis. This provision may also erode another mainframe advantage, the facility for multistream batch processing.

Mainframes, it is proposed, will continue to exist, but only for massive single stream computations ('in 10 years' time . . . the commercial mainframe will have ceased to exist' – Healey).

Another approach to the enhancement of micro power is a configuration, common with minicomputers, in which a central master CPU is shared between several workstations, each with its own slave CPU. When micros exploit this sort of provision they can achieve computing power, speed and flexibility at least equivalent to what can be found in small minicomputer systems. A typical configuration of this sort is Jarogate's MP5 multi-user multiprocessor micro in which up to 16 slave CPUs (one for each user) and a master CPU are linked together by a high-speed, 16-bit parallel network.

The growing power of micros is not only affecting the role of the larger stand-alone systems. There is also an impact on the relatively unsophisticated dumb terminals – on, for example, the simple CRT terminal. Some observers suggest that the increasing popularity of microcomputers has already dented the market for CRT terminals that lack local processing capability. As LSI costs drop, there will be little incentive for manufacturers to provide terminals without processing power (one analyst has already remarked that 'there are really no dumb terminals any more'), and one consequence will be a blurring of the distinction between terminals and microcomputers – low-end micros will be much the same, in terms of both price and performance, as high-end terminals.

16-bit microcomputers are already ousting 8-bit micros and starting to acquire minicomputer performance, and 32-bit micros are already available. For example the powerful Motorola 68000 micro, the main rival to Intel's 8086/8 family, has a 32-bit internal architecture and can address 16M bytes of memory. A cut-down version, the 68008, is used in the Sinclair QL.

Perhaps most remarkably, an advanced version, the 68020, will soon be available. This micro has a 32-bit data bus and can address

4G bytes (four thousand million bytes) of memory. Moreover it is intended to run at 16.67MHz, and so perform around 2.5 million instructions per second. In one estimate (Schofield, 1985) a 68020-based micro will be able to provide about 97 per cent of the power of a mainframe computer at around 3 per cent of the cost; and such a system could be available within the next two or three years.

Technology

Advances in microcomputer design and the consequent availability of an ever larger spectrum of applications software are rapidly expanding the base of potential micro users. For example, in UK engineering plants 62 per cent of around 15,000 installed computers were micros in 1983, with 72 per cent of nearly 28,000 installed systems in 1984 (Potts, 1984). Minis and mainframes have dropped to 22 and 6 per cent respectively though actual numbers have increased. Moreover the trends that are evident in engineering can also be detected in other industrial, commercial and service sectors. Progress in micro technology is expanding the applications spectrum and the base of potential users.

The development of large-scale integration, a key factor in the evolution of microcomputers, has affected such factors as density of information storage and the size of CPUs. For instance, we saw a 1K RAM in 1970, a 16K RAM in 1976, and a 256K chip in 1984 (with a 1M bit chip expected in 1985). A number of advances have contributed to this pace of development. The growing of silicon crystals has improved, allowing the generation of large fault-free areas; and greater packing densities have been obtained by means of improved mask production using electron beam techniques. Computers themselves have assisted with circuit board layout tasks and with many other aspects of design. Chip manufacture has been aided by increased automation, allowing, for example, the production of chips in superior dust-free environments uncontaminated by human beings. The development of superior microprocessors has been stimulated by the growing involvement of computer-based facilities in the various design and fabrication processes.

Many of the new micros are dubbed 'advanced microcomputers'

or 'supermicros'.* Invariably they represent dramatic improvements over other micros from the same stable. Thus the Personal Computer AT from IBM – featuring the Intel 80286 microprocessor, a high-capacity diskette drive, and expanded disk drive options – gives almost five times the user memory and more than twice the information storage capacity previously available on IBM personal computers. The AT remains compatible with most IBM PC hardware and software, and can be used by one person or shared by up to three.

Another micro striving after minicomputer power is the MicroPDP-11/73 which offers performance comparable to that of a PDP-11/44 model. This microcomputer, based on the J-11 microprocessor, features the same enclosure, power supply and Q-bus architecture as the microVAX and the less powerful MicroPDP-11/23. Hence the entire family of Q-bus peripherals and mass storage devices is available to the new micro. The MicroPDP-11/73 is intended to compete with 68000- and 286-based microcomputers, and for this reason many different configurations are available.

Competitive pressures may also have influenced the IBM launch of the Baby 36 supermicro, only a few days after AT & T announced the 3B2 supermicro. It has been suggested that IBM speeded up development to prevent the likelihood of AT & T gaining a foothold. Systems of this type are usually intended for multi-user, multi-tasking office sites, and commonly exploit existing operating systems. The supermicro – by virtue of its large storage capacity, shared databases, and the ability to run sophisticated applications software – is attracting increasing attention. IRD has predicted that there will be a growth from the 52,500 sales in 1983 to around 850,000 units per year in 1993 (to a value of $5.4 million).

The IBM and AT & T innovations may damage the market prospects for other supermicro makers, such as Tandy, Altos Computer Systems and Fortune Systems. AT & T will have difficulty confronting IBM's commercial success in the personal-computer market. Moreover there are hints of strain between AT

* See, for example, the survey of supermicros in *Which Computer?*, February 1985.

& T and Olivetti who distribute AT & T computers in Europe. One scenario is that AT & T could crumble in Europe, and Olivetti, with its plans to introduce an IBM PC-compatible micro, could fail in the US.

The growing abilities of microcomputers, in whatever market sector, will attract an ever larger user base interested in a rapidly expanding applications spectrum. Technological progress will affect not only machine performance but also such factors as 'upgradeability' and user-friendliness. New input facilities will overcome, for example, the reluctance of some senior managers to become involved in keyboarding (see, for example, Newman, 1984); and other evolutionary characteristics will emerge via the various AI and fifth-generation programmes. Already there is a non-von Neumann type microprocessor available from NEC, able to handle vast volumes of image and numerical data (alternatives to von Neumann architectures are often seen as key fifth-generation innovations).

NEC's μPD7281D Image Pipelined Processor is promoted as a superchip, the world's first practical data-flow VSLI architecture. (For example, the micro spins a 512 x 512-pixel binary image in 1.4 seconds, and carries out a 3 x 3 masking on a 512 x 512-pixel gray -scale image in 2.9 seconds. Multiprocessing can cut execution time dramatically.) This micro enlarges the scope of image-recognition systems, facsimiles, etc and offers new possibilities for applications in other fields. The Inmos 'transputer' is another development deemed to herald the fifth generation of computer systems.

Inmos unveiled the transputer, a 32-bit microprocessor, in late-1983 with the expectation that the new product would face stiff competition from other companies. It was known that Motorola, Intel, Digital Equipment and Bell Laboratories were preparing 32-bit processor chips, and Hewlett-Packard and National Semiconductor were already making them. The transputer was designed with 4K bytes of static random-access memory (RAM), and to allow information to be shuttled between this memory and the processor fast enough for program instructions to be carried out at the rate of 10 million per second. The small size of the transputer – 45 square millimetres compared to a typical 100 mm² for other products – also assists the rapid processing of information.

In one estimate (Iann Barron), development costs are around £5 million; Hewlett-Packard spent $100 million on producing its 32-bit μprocessor. The Inmos unveiling of the 32-bit transputer followed announcements from other companies: AT & T (the Bellmac 32), Hewlett-Packard (the MCS III), Intel (the 432), NCR (the NCR-200), and DEC (the MicroVAX I). The current plans are for the transputer (see detailed description in Barron et al, 1983) to go into full production in late-1985.

The increased power of micro-based systems is facilitating a progressive migration of functions from mainframes to micros. Tasks formerly limited to large systems can now be performed efficiently on microcomputers. One example is how graphics can be handled by the new breeds of supermicros. Dr Michael Glazer (of the Clarendon Physics Laboratory in Oxford), as one user, has acquired an Orion supermicro to help in work on crystal structures. Here it is necessary to plot images from calculations on as many as 10,000 readings obtained by passing X-rays or neutrons through crystalline materials. It is significant that the scope of the super-micro in this context apparently exceeds that of many larger systems. Thus Glazer observes: 'We just wouldn't be able to do it [if forced to rely on the university's mainframes]. We couldn't hold our data files on the VAX (Digital Equipment's biggest minicomputer) or the 2900 (an ICL mainframe)' (quoted by Lamb, 1984).

This example illustrates a general trend in scientific, industrial and other fields. It is becoming increasingly convenient to perform tasks on micro-based systems that would formerly have been confined to mainframes and minicomputers. There are obvious cost savings, and dedicated micros are often convenient and more appropriate for specific applications. We do not always appreciate just how far the migration of functions has progressed, but this is clearly a trend that will continue and have implications for expert systems and other AI-related software.

Migration of Functions

From the early-1970s the developing potential of micro-based systems has been evident. The early mainframes of the 1950s were soon found to be suitable for playing chess and other games, but the later micros quickly became interested. The first microcomputer chess championships were held in California in 1978, and by 1984 it was possible to run AI chess programs on micros. For example, the Mephisto program, far removed from a crude brute-force approach, aims for a pre-selective, intelligent search and in-depth analysis (Harrington, 1983). It makes four brute force moves but then follows them by four selective moves, allowing an eight-ply searching sequence. Such a program can surprise a human player with its moves. Moreover since the intelligent search approach implies a more 'intuitive', humanlike mode of play, the machine can play brilliantly one day and badly the next. Mephisto is one of many programs that suggest that it is not unreasonable to expect microcomputers to behave in an intelligent fashion.

At the same time it is clear that large computers, with massive storage capacities, can have advantages over micros. Again this can be illustrated from the world of chess (Watt, 1984). In a recent international competition, micros played supercomputers but made few inroads. At one stage the 6502-based Fidelity Experimental system faced the multimillion-dollar defending champion, the Cray Blitz. The micro contained some 16,000 opening combinations, compared with the Cray's capacity for around 100,000 openings. Fidelity programmer Dan Spracklen commented: 'The Cray Blitz opened with a move that wasn't in our book. It went downhill from there'.

The successes of micro-based systems, in game playing and elsewhere, has stimulated increased interest in the generation of software for the proliferating number of users of small computer systems. This was shown by, for example, the range of entries for the 1984 British Computer Society awards, organised in conjunction with *Computing* (see Sheridan, 1984). Here we saw programs for remodelling road accidents, for 'teleshopping', for aiding medical practice, for exploiting database facilities, etc. Already there are expert-systems programs able to run on micros (see Expert Systems, below, and Chapter 5) and we may expect rapid development in this area.

We have already touched on the emergence of decision-support software for micros and how this is related to the development of expert systems. Software suppliers have been influenced by, for instance, the availability of VisiCalc on Apple micros. Comshare and other companies have been encouraged by the success of such packages as VisiCalc and Lotus 1-2-3, marketed as decision support systems, to look at the micro software scene and to develop appropriate products. Such developments mirror what is happening in many applications areas. We have noticed, for example, the increasing use of micro-based systems in engineering.

One survey (Atkin, 1984) suggests that 60% of UK engineering companies that employ less than 500 people are now using microcomputers, and we may assume extensive usage in larger organisations. The survey finds that particular micros tend to be used in particular applications:

— draughting (ACT Sirius, IBM PCs and XTs, PETs);

— testing (Apples, BBC Micros);

— costing and estimating (PETs);

— electronic testing (Apples, PETs);

— process planning (ACT Sirius, Apples);

— NC and CNC programming (BBCs, ACT Sirius and Apricots, Epson, Olivetti and Hewlett-Packard micros).

Many micro-based applications in the engineering environment are routine (for example, straightforward administration and file management), but it is obvious that increasingly sophisticated tasks, once the sole province of mainframes, are now being carried out on micros. Computer-aided design, modelling, simulations, etc are typical examples.

A computer-aided design facility, the Draft-Aide system introduced by United Networking Systems Inc, is available for the IBM Personal Computer XT. (Thomas Safford and David Lowman, president and vice-president of the company, are convinced that micros are the key to the future of computer-aided design.) The Draft-Aide facility is offered in six versions, three of which are intended for engineers, architects and draughting professionals. The other versions (Starter 100, Academic 100 and System 300) can individually be used as instructional aids and for other pur-

THE MICROCOMPUTER ADVANCE

poses. The company intends to develop versions of Draft-Aide for other microcomputers.

The increasing use of micro-based facilities is evident in many industrial, commercial, service and domestic environments. The following examples, which could easily be extended, are taken at random from the literature:

— Voice mail systems are being integrated with personal computers. The research firm, Venture Development Corporation, counts more than 28 vendors vying for a share of the voice-technology market, and at least three companies are expected to exploit the expected boom (estimate of sales of $2.3 billion in 1987) by building voice mail expansion boards for IBM Personal Computers. Howitt (1984): '. . . new systems for personal computers have managed to incorporate most of the tricks of minicomputer-based voice mail'. The IBM PC voice mail system, the PC Dial Log supplied as an IBM PC expansion board, is now widely distributed in US computer stores. The system can hold a telephone list of 200 names and numbers and dial them automatically. It can call people, play a message, and record responses. It can also ask callers for an identification number and recognise encounters with another PC Dial Log;

— A complete personnel system can now be incorporated in a microcomputer. Thus Comshare has designed the Profiles/PC package for IBM's hard-disk personal computer, the XT. The system is suitable for companies with less than 2000 employees, but can also be used at a divisional or departmental level in larger organisations. Profiles/PC can also be linked to an in-house or bureau mainframe for handling information at corporate level;

— Simulation software can now run on micros. For example, the ISIM facility can be used for diverse applications (eg the design of satellite control systems, the study of the human body's blood system). Two phases are involved in the simulation: the formation of a mathematical model, comprising differential and algebraic equations; and the simulation (solution) of the model, allowing experiments to be performed on the model rather than on the physical system. ISIS is an extended version for minicomputers. ISIM/ISIS, used extensively in the UK and elsewhere, runs on most micros and minicomputers, including:

— IBM PC and PC/XT with 128K memory;

— DEC Rainbow, Apple with Z80 card;

— CP/M 8-bit micros with 44K memory;

— CP/M 86 16-bit micros with 128K memory;

— MS/DOS micros with 128K memory;

— PRIME, DEC PDP-11 and VAX, SEL, Perkin Elmer, Harris, Norsk Data, HP.

The results are often presented graphically using the micro's built-in graphics or Tektronix-compatible graphics terminals. The highly interactive nature of ISIM/ISIS makes it a powerful simulation tool (Crosbie, 1984);

— Forecasting systems, available on micros, are now being supplied for various purposes. For example, Automatic Forecasting Systems Inc has introduced microcomputer versions of several of its mainframe forecasting packages: Autobj, Autobox, Box and Simulator. The software, available for an IBM Personal Computer with 256K bytes of internal memory and two diskette drives, allows users to build univariate and multivariate Box-Jenkins models, including intervention models. The system can also allow users to identify, estimate and forecast, without using the product's automatic features;

— Micros are increasingly able to handle speech phenomena, ie to cope with the relatively easy speech synthesis and the much more difficult speech (or voice) recognition (or understanding). In one application (Cote, 1983), an experimental speech input card was used to enable an IBM Personal Computer to plot the sounds of vowels. Such facilities could be developed to serve as speech training aids for the deaf;

— Natural-language understanding is now increasingly within

the reach of micro-based systems. For example, during 1984, programs able to use natural-language queries for data retrieval appeared in microcomputer shops. Bond (1984) suggests that this type of query facility – whereby a computer understands and responds to questions asked in normal syntax using a normal vocabulary – first appeared on micros in Versafile, designed in the late-1970s to run on the TRS-80 Model 1. CLOUT, produced recently by MicroRIM Inc, is an add-on program designed to manipulate databases and to run on micros;

— We have already seen (in Fedanzo, 1984) that versions of Cobol can run on micros. It is worth emphasising that particular applications are relevant in this context. For example, most batch data entry systems are suitable candidate applications for distributed data processing (DDP) using micros. This covers a range of systems – from those that simply accept input from a CRT and pass it to a plain file, to those that perform on-line validation of key items. Fedanzo gives a flowchart to indicate a general procedure for determining whether an application is a likely candidate for conversion to microprocessor DDP. This approach is applicable, *mutatis mutandis*, to other types of tasks performed on mainframes but being considered for down loading onto micros;

— Increasingly we see claims about the capacity of micro-based systems to handle database-related functions. Research by Intelligent Electronics showed that in the UK, 30% of companies surveyed have connected at least one of their personal computers to a database. There is a similar proportion in West Germany, with only 9% in France. Today we often see database software offered for micros, though there is debate about its effectiveness. Thus VIM (versatile information manager) is a database management system, designed to run on the TRS-80, that helps in the organisation and retrieval of information; Infocom Inc has introduced a relational database program for IBM Personal Computers; and Superfile is a database management package for storing information on microcomputers. However, of the many micro software packages only a few provide true database management facilities. Gooding (1983) explores various packages (MDBS, FMS-80, DMS, dBase II, Rescue and Superfile) under the appropriate heading, 'How to Squeeze a Quart into a Pint Pot'. It has also been pointed out that even the new 16-bit micros do not handle large databases very efficiently, and that micro software in this area should be dubbed 'single user';

— Word processing software is increasingly available for micros but here too there is debate about its effectiveness. In *Data Processing* (October 1984), we find that 'WP systems lose to PCs'. It is noted that there is rapid growth with personal computers dedicated to word processing (growth of 120% in one year to total 25,000 installations in Europe). However it is noted that most WP packages are clumsy and the operating systems slow. The Wharton Information Systems report suggests that transporting software from dedicated word processors to personal computers should not be too difficult, and that the challenge to word processors will grow as the quality of PC screens and keyboards improves. Samish (1984/85) discusses why the micro has not succeeded in displacing the dedicated word processor. The situation is one we have met elsewhere – micros are making impressive gains but media hype, leading to overselling, is still too common;

— Microcomputer software is now available to serve as program generators (Ash, 1983; Chard, 1985). The demise of the human programmer is prematurely predicted but the various program generators, used properly, can aid the programming task in various ways.

The scope of microcomputers is being enlarged in various ways. With larger available memories and more powerful processing capabilities, micros are now challenging mainframes in some application areas. In addition, new applications – which may not have been thought of without the advent of the micro – are being developed. With micros able to perform, with varying degrees of efficiency, such applications as computer-aided design, voice-mail handling, personnel management, modelling and simulation, voice recognition, natural-language understanding, database management and word processing, the challenge to large systems is obvious. In such circumstances we should expect significant micro gains in other areas traditionally dominated by mainframes and top-end minicomputers.

Expert systems and other AI products were around before the first microcomputers but, in this field also, micros are beginning to stake their claim. Before looking in more detail at the spectrum of expert systems, and at micro companies and products, it is worth indicating some current connections between micros and artificial intelligence (see Chapter 5 for details of some micro-based expert systems and related products).

MICROS AND AI

The migration of functions from mainframes to microcomputers is discernible in the area of artificial intelligence, as it is evident elsewhere; and specific AI-related programs are being designed for micros. In recent years it has become increasingly practical to implement intelligent software on small machines, though companies developing such programs are still likely to carry out much of their work on large machines. Again it is worth mentioning the debate in this area. For example, with regard to expert systems on micros, Watt (1984) points out that many of the products claiming to be AI-aided expert systems 'rely on mathematical matching principles rather than intelligence'. 'True AI' is still rare on micros, as perhaps it is elsewhere.

Moves to make artificial intelligence more practical on microcomputers include providing suitable language versions for small systems. This is noticeable with the migration of dialects of Lisp and Prolog, the main AI languages (some hobbyists are keen to show how Basic can be used for expert systems). For example, Gold Hill Computers has introduced Golden Common Lisp which adapts DARPA's Common Lisp for personal computers; and Silogic Inc has provided a Prolog compiler for microcomputers. Most working micros, it has to be said, have little interest in the main AI languages. A survey run recently by *Electronic Design* (29 November 1984) showed that Lisp was the most popular language for only 3% of engineering users of personal computers. At the same time there is a growing family of expert systems, of debatable competence, for microcomputers (see Chapter 5).

Clive Sinclair has discussed the possibility of expert systems for his products; the IBM Personal Computer now has shells for expert systems to allow dedicated systems to be developed for specific purposes; and Acorn, supplier of the BBC Microcomputer, recently announced that advisory systems would be available to help with particular problems – for example, medical diagnosis. And as the suppliers of machines look to how they can provide AI-related programs for their hardware products, so the software suppliers are exploring how to provide expert systems for available commercial micros. In some cases a system has been developed in a Lisp-based environment and then, to save processing time, ported to either Basic (for example, Puff, the pulmonary diagnostic program developed by Stanford and UCSF) or Forth (for example, Delta/Cats, a locomotive diagnostic program developed by General Electric). Both of these systems run on a small PDP-11, and in early-1985 Delta/Cats was being made available for the IBM Personal Computer.

IBM is also said to be developing an expert-system shell in Pascal. Here it may be possible to develop a consultation style expert system on a computer with a memory of 128K to 256K bytes. Various devices can be adopted to reduce the computation demands: it has been emphasised that consultation-type systems spend more time waiting for user input than performing computations. Disk facilities are less important than may be thought – mainly because many expert systems load the data and production rules into memory before they begin to operate. Most of the new start-up companies are targeting IBM Personal Computers as the likely hardware for micro-based expert systems. This trend could lead to hand-held expert systems that could be used at work or at home to work out tax and accounting problems, to perform medical and car diagnosis, and to offer advice in many other areas. The implications of such cheap and widespread expertise have yet to be fully appreciated.

In late-1984 a 'full-time psychologist in the form of an expert system' was released in Australia (Garnett, 1984). The system developed by, and imported from, the US company Human Edge software, is intended for salesmen. Divided into four modules –

communications, negotiations, sales and management – the package enables the user to evaluate the personalities involved in negotiations and suggests suitable tactics in a competitive situation. The program requires the user to rate the intended customer by agreeing or not with fifty adjectives (such as kind, sarcastic, outgoing, etc), whereupon the program generates an eight to 10-page report including comments on 'what to expect' and 'how to succeed', as well as detailed strategies linked to what is thought to be the customer's psyche. In effect the program classifies both the salesman and the customer into one of 12 different personality types, and then generates advice accordingly.

The package was released in September 1984 and twenty modules were soon sold in Australia (with projected 1985 sales of around 1000). One problem, according to Alex Babauskis, managing director of the distributing company Taylor & Stewart Computer Services, is that the package is too Americanised ('By early next year [1985], after we get the source code, we hope to Australise it, and have a version available for the DEC Rainbow micro').

There is some doubt, of course, that such a package embodies 'true-AI' techniques. The smaller the target computer the greater the space constraint, though we have seen how an expert system (Puff) written for a large computer has been rewritten in Basic and shoehorned into a micro. Many specialists still believe that expert systems proper are beyond the scope of micros. Thus Alexander Jacobson, president of Inference in Los Angeles, has commented: 'We don't think any expert system worthy of the name can run on a micro'. To carry out automatic problem solving using automatic inferencing on a knowledge base is, it is suggested, beyond the capacity of modern micros. Gerrold Kaplan, chief development officer of Teknowledge in Palo Alto, California, similarly doubts that some of the current commercial products are true expert systems, but nonetheless declares: 'I see a bright future for knowledge systems on microcomputers' (quoted by Watt, *Infoworld*, 23/4/84).

In a similar vein, Johnson (1984), surveying the commercial possibilities, declares that the best prospects are for 'packages running on personal computers for use by the experts themselves'. One key implication is that small systems 'are likely to attract sharply increased attention in the next year or two, with some early commercial successes'. Moreover there will be frequent resort to the expert-system approach for reasons of convenience – 'and at least partly for its novelty and glamour'. The new systems will signal a real advance in the scope of computer capabilities.

There are a growing number of suppliers offering expert system shells to run on microcomputers; most of these, as we have seen, are aimed at the IBM PC. Such shells, too modest for the development of substantial systems, are sometimes exploited to aid management decision making and the development of other systems. One of the first of these systems was MicroExpert from Isis Systems in the UK. Among the many others are APES and ES/P Advisor, both written in Prolog; Expert-Ease, written in Pascal; and M.1 from Teknowledge, sold by Framentec in Europe. APES, developed by Peter Hammond and Marek Sergot at Imperial College, will be marketed by their new company, Logic Based Systems. Again it will be aimed at IBM PCs and similar machines. (This package and others are described in more detail in Chapter 5.)

The various commercial micro-based expert systems are usually based on experimental research systems. For example, Kowalski and colleagues at Imperial College have demonstrated a small expert system running on a micro, in this case exploiting a 150-rule knowledge base covering a section of the British Nationality Act on a 128K byte IBM Personal Computer (the full knowledge base, appropriate for a larger machine, has 500 rules). This system may be expected to have commercial implications.

Other micro-based expert systems are already employed in fault-diagnosis applications. General Electric's Cats-1, for instance, is being employed in diesel locomotive maintenance; a system has been developed by British Telecom for testing 11 GHz radio equipment; and SPL International is using a system for field maintenance of electronic equipment.

Expert systems for such (and other) purposes can be developed on a large machine, and then compiled into algorithmic form in a conventional language. Rutgers University have adopted this approach for a system developed with the World Health Authority for primary eye care. The system, employing a 131-rule knowledge base, has been compiled into Basic to run on an Apple IIe micro and, in a more limited version, on an Epson HX-20 micro. With this approach the resulting product may not be a true expert system, but the expert system at a higher level may be exploited to yield useful microcomputer software.

We may expect the micro-based expert systems of the future to be capable of running Lisp or Prolog. Johnson (1984) suggests that the first-generation delivery vehicle will have up to 1M byte of memory as standard (and will need to sell for less than $10,000 in the US). Current research – funded by Alvey, Esprit, DARPA, the Japanese fifth-generation programme, etc – has implications for the emergence of AI facilities, including expert systems, on micros. The convergence of increasing microcomputer power and real AI software will have a growing impact on the market scene. Micro-based facilities will be economically available in commerce, industry and other environments; and cheap advisory and consultation provisions will be commonplace. The shake-out predicted for the micro marketplace for 1985 and beyond will leave fewer micro-product companies in the arena, but their offerings will continue to progress in technological terms. It is likely that micro-based AI will be very widespread in the years ahead.

THE MICRO FUTURE

Microcomputers, of ever increasing power, will proliferate in the years to come. A 1984 survey from International Data Corporation suggests that there will be an international installed base of personal computers of nearly sixteen million in 1989 (compared with 3,588,000 in 1985). Micros, via various networks and links, will be increasingly involved in communications functions. And the human/machine interface will evolve to be less evident, more natural. This implies, for example, that voice recognition will be a commonplace feature of microcomputers (Hunter, 1984): we may, in the longer term, expect micros to become intelligent conversationalists.

Attention is being given to how microcomputers can be linked to mainframes, a development stimulated by the rapid growth in the number of personal computers in the corporate environment (see, for example, Phillips, 1984). In this way, micro users can gain access to large databases for spreadsheet, report generation and other applications. There will be ways in which microcomputers will be able to tap the AI resources of larger systems. The requirement for remote micro networks (Presley, 1984) is a related topic, relevant to how small systems can function together by means of appropriate communications links. (The computing/communications convergence is evident here as elsewhere.)

Many observers suggest that artificial-intelligence developments will greatly influence how micros will look in the future. Thus Juliussen (1984) identifies three key technologies that will shape the personal computers of 1990:

— software based on AI technology;

— mass storage devices based on optical disks;

— flat display technologies.

It is noted that AI products are currently available on mainframe computers, but that 'personal computers will be the major market for these products'. The specific processing and storage requirements of AI systems will act as a stimulus to micro development.

Various categories of optical read-write disks are projected for the future personal computer industry. Similarly, flat displays will improve substantially in the next few years, and will contribute to the evolution of battery-powered personal computers (with LCD in the lead because of its low power consumption). The various developments are expected to lead to a floppy disk personal computer with at least 4M bytes of RAM by 1990. A colour graphics display will be standard, as will a multifunction printer. And it is also suggested (by Juliussen) that the primary software will be 'integrated productivity programs that have been enhanced by AI technologies'. Various other parallel developments for micros in the office, the home and other environments may be expected. Anderson (1984) suggests that it is easy to predict what will happen on the micro hardware front.

There will be moves to develop powerful 16-, 32- and 64-bit CPU chips that will require little voltage and operate at very high speeds (10 MHz+). Increasingly complete circuits – comprising, for example, one or more central processors and multiple support processors – will be etched as a single chip. Memories will become cheaper and less bulky. A 3.5″ hard disk drive capable of storing 20M bytes will emerge, and the 1.5″ floppy will be able to carry 1M byte per side. Full-screen colour LCDs will become available, and inevitably there will be dramatic strides in miniaturisation ('By 1990 no computer bigger than the Apple Macintosh will be selling well').

With regard to software, Anderson predicts that such phrases and words as *ease of use, integration,* and software that works *intuitively* will not fade from fashion, Perhaps here we can detect hints of AI. The easiest predictions are the most banal. Chips will become denser, cheaper, more powerful, etc. With software there are perhaps fewer easy extrapolations from current trends, but most observers (eg Pournelle, 1983) predict that software will be cheaper, more universal, and easier to use. Voice control frequently crops up in the predictions, and it is emphasised that a lot of software is now being written in Lisp (there is some criticism of the Japanese fifth-generation programme for relying on Prolog as the kernel language). In this connection, Pournelle declares: 'A lot of artificial intelligence people will suddenly be able to write programs with a potential market of tens of thousands of copies'.

Again we frequently find that micros will rival larger systems. Parallel processing will overcome the problems associated with single chips ('Concurrent CP/M-86 is just now catching on; when people realise just what you can do with concurrent processing, it will really take off'). In the future we are likely to see several CPUs available to every user, with micro-based systems cheaper, easier to use, and more like traditional larger systems in performance potential.

SUMMARY

This chapter has highlighted aspects of the international micro scene to indicate important trends and developments. We have noted the growing significance of micro-based systems and how functions formerly restricted to mainframes are progressively migrating to micros. The anticipated shake-out amongst microcomputer makers has been mentioned and also some aspects of the current commercial scene.

A key development, for our purposes, is the provision of AI-related software for micros. This can occur in various ways. Main-frame systems can be trimmed down for micros (we have seen that the Puff expert system was compiled into Basic for use on micros), or programs can be designed from scratch for use on personal computers and other small systems. At the same time we have discerned the persistent reservations about the scope of micro-computers in an AI context.

The growing power of the micro is one of the most important developments in the international computer scene. There is little doubt that its scope is increasing dramatically, almost month by month. This trend is occasioned by various parallel developments – new fabrication techniques, new integration technologies, new modes of parallel (or concurrent) processing, new software methods and languages, etc. The emerging families of micros will continue to encroach on the traditional realms of minicomputers and mainframes (we have seen one pundit predict the demise of the mainframe within ten years).

In these circumstances of growing micro competence there will be few functions that will remain the sole province of large main-frame systems: parallel configurations of powerful micros will be able to compete. If AI and AI-related functions are realistic appli-cations on mainframe computers, it will be increasingly difficult to argue that artificial intelligence is not a legitimate interest of microcomputers. In such an analysis, the current state of (mainly) mainframe-related expert systems is clearly relevant to how AI will be increasingly realised on micros.

3 The Spectrum of Expert Systems*

INTRODUCTION

Doubts, in some circles, about the claims of AI-related products stand in marked contrast to the increasing proliferation of expert systems. Today it is easy to find 'expert systems' being explored in almost every discipline, in almost every industrial and commercial sector. This should not be taken to imply that all the product claims are equally valid. There is in fact immense variation among what are declared by suppliers to be true expert systems, to 'contain AI'. Expert systems vary in size, application field and general competence. Some programs embody no discernible AI features but steal some of the glamour of artificial intelligence and (true) expert systems by being described in the fashionable AI language. This chapter profiles the wide spectrum of expert systems without any attempt to explore the claims made for particular products.

Expert systems often overlap other families of software that may not have AI pretensions. We have already noticed this (see Chapter 1) in connection with ideas processors, decision support systems, etc. Most expert systems are reckoned to be problem solvers, but a problem solver (eg TK!Solver, see Daniel, 1983) is not necessarily an expert system. True expert systems have a number of characteristic features. For example, they work with a knowledge base in a particular field, drawing inferences in one way or another, assigning probability ratings to conclusions that are derived, and providing the user with a 'window' into the various

---

* This chapter is based partly on Chapter 8 from *Introducing Artificial Intelligence* (NCC Publications, 1984).

85

inference procedures. Not all the expert systems profiled here have all these features, but some of these characteristics, or closely analogous ones, can be found in them all.

THE EXPERT SYSTEMS RANGE

Expert systems, of one sort or another, are now beginning to be used in countless industrial, commercial, service, domestic and military environments. But not all of these systems are equally successful. It has been suggested that systems will tend to group in specific 'islands' where the commercial factors are particularly favourable. These applications islands are shown, in a much simplified form, in Figure 3.1. Johnson (1984) suggests that the most promising islands for developing expert systems are in:

— *computing, electronics and communications:* fault diagnosis and maintenance; expert front ends; design and configuration systems;

— *oil exploration and extraction:* fault diagnosis and trouble shooting; analysis of seismic data;

— *financial services:* sales and management support; portfolio management;

— *military applications:* fault diagnosis and maintenance; expert front ends; training.

These key sectors, explored below, all require considerable funding from governments and private organisations. At the same time, successful ventures in such fields are likely to be immensely lucrative. Software houses and other suppliers will tend to concentrate on specific applications sectors that look promising, and with these companies too there will be inevitable shake-outs as excessive product claims are exposed and as successful enterprises manage to secure particular corners of the market.

The current funded research programmes (Chapter 1) have implications for expert systems in all application sectors. For example, the Japanese fifth-generation programme is directly relevant to work on expert systems. The key work in this connection focuses on such topics as inference software, user friendliness

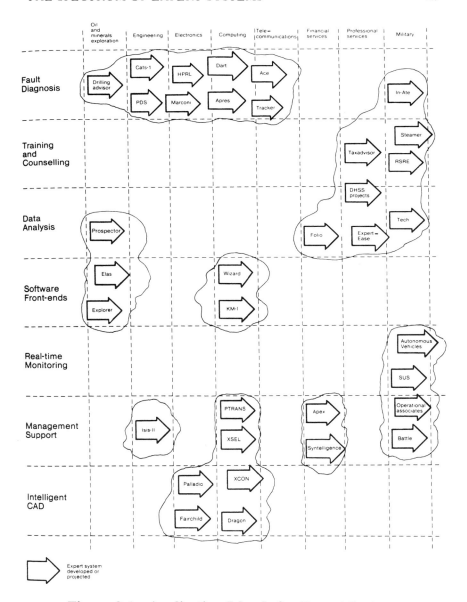

Figure 3.1   Application Islands for Expert Systems
(Source: Johnson, 1984)

(the man/machine interface), and techniques for knowledge representation. Current Japanese work on expert systems (see Ishizuka, 1984) is directed at:

— *Medical diagnosis and consultation*
  Recent projects have included the development of a medical consultation system, MECS-AI, for cardiovascular diseases (Kaihara et al at the University of Tokyo); the ANTICIPATOR consultation system for the selection of antibiotics (Kaihara et al); a consultation system for glaucoma (Mizoguchi at the Science University of Tokyo); and a consultation system, μ-RHEUM, for rheumatism;

— *Plant surveillance and control*
  Such companies as Hitachi, Mitsubishi and Toshiba are interested in developing expert systems for the surveillance and control of large plants. Motoda and Yamada (at Hitachi's Energy Research Laboratory) are developing a system for the surveillance of a nuclear power plant; and Sakaguchi et al (at Mitsubishi's Central Laboratory) are also building an expert system to control an electric power facility;

— *Industrial damage assessment*
  Ishizuka (at the University of Tokyo) has developed an expert system, SPERIL-I, for structural damage assessment. This system exploits a variety of fuzzy logic and inference techniques. An enhanced version, SPERIL-II, has been developed by Ogawa (at Purdue University);

— *Management and office systems*
  Hitachi's System Development Laboratory is developing various expert systems in this field: for example, a system for making cost estimates, and a frame system for managing warehouses. Higashida et al have produced a prototype system for an 'intelligent secretary' which manages the schedules of personnel in a company. At ICOT, an expert system for proofreading Japanese texts is being developed;

— *Computer-aided design*
  Kawato et al (at Fujitsu) are developing a new logic design system able to exploit AI techniques. Major tasks in this

context are logic synthesis and verification under a description of logic circuit specification. Goto et al (NEC) are developing an automatic circuit routeing system. Expert systems are also being developed in the areas of electrical CAD, mechanical CAD, architectural CAD, etc (see below);

— *Image processing*
Expert systems in this area have a wide field of potential application (for example, in engineering and medical consultation). Tamura et al (Electrotechnical Laboratory) have developed the SPIDER image processing program, and the DIA-Expert system is being developed to act as an advisor in the use of SPIDER. Various groups are also exploring knowledge-based computer vision systems;

— *Database access*
Mizoguchi et al (Osaka University) are developing a user-friendly interface for database purposes.*

The various Japanese initiatives have stimulated research elsewhere in the world, but it is also the case that work on expert systems in, say, the US predated in many instances the Japanese activities. US research in this field has been going on for two or three decades, and the Japanese continue to derive benefits from this source. Shaw (1983), discussing a five-day conference of the American Association for Artificial Intelligence (AAAI), cites various examples of AI activity in the United States:

— General Electric has developed an expert system, CATS-1, for diagnosing faults in locomotive engines. Use is made of a PDP-11/23 processor;

— DEC has developed the XSEL expert system, used successfully in-house to help sales staff to define system configurations for customers;

— Symbolics Inc is marketing its 3600 symbolic processing system for use as an R&D tool to develop AI expert sys-

---

* See bibliography in Ishizuka (1984) for references to articles describing the work mentioned in this section.

tems. Customers already include Bell, GE, Mitre and Fairchild;

— Interface Corp has introduced the ART inference engine that can be combined with knowledge bases to construct a variety of expert systems. CDC is using ART in product development.

In addition to these specific, well publicised products work is continuing in many different fields: robotics, office automation, medicine, military applications, etc. In these and other areas academic research is being directed towards the development of practical commercial products: for example, the use of expert systems with database management facilities is receiving considerable attention. At the First International Workshop on Expert Data Base Systems, held in Washington in late-1984, researchers from universities and the business sector discussed how to use AI query and inference techniques to manage complex database management systems (DBMS). A consensus emerged that in the years to come large databases will need built-in logic aids to help programmers working with the data. Dr Larry Kerschberg observed: 'Databases, while they are good at storing facts, have not generally been able to apply rules that are based on reasoning and inferences. We are trying to extend the concept of expert systems to handle databases'.

In this context expert systems can rely upon experience to update their knowledge base, and they can perform this task by deleting redundancies and inaccuracies. Ideally they can also explain to the human user what they are up to. However at present it seems clear that expert systems require considerable computing power whereas DBMS are more economical in computing and searching. Expert systems can offer modes of inferential searching not available in DBMS, but it should be established that such modes are required before an expensive merging of DBMS and expert systems is attempted.

A wide range of expert-systems research is being conducted with a view to commercial return (see below). Some of the work focuses on diagnosis of faults in electronic circuits, design tasks in structural engineering, assessment of investment risks, and evaluation of social-security entitlements in the US (for example, using the

Demsoc expert system developed by the Rand Corporation). Wherever advice or consultancy is required, there is scope for the use of expert systems, and they can also be used directly in the investigation of AI-related problems (eg problems associated with speech synthesis).

Researchers at the Centre National d'Etudes des Télécommunications (CNET) in Lannion, Brittany, have developed an expert system called Synthex (to denote System Synthesis Expert). The system is intended to use AI techniques to study the problems involved in synthesising speech from a written text and in formalising the resulting knowledge for use in practical applications. Synthex relies on synthesis by diphones (a pair of phonemes, the smallest significant units of speech) and uses prosody (manipulations of duration, loudness, and pitch). To enable computer-naive researchers to use Synthex, a facility is included whereby the operator can enter commands in a quasi-natural language. The system (outlined by Gallagher, 1985) currently runs on a 16-bit multi-user SM 90 computer.

Other expert-systems work is concerned with helping robots to become intelligent. Since robots will need to interpret the information provided by visual, tactile and other sensors, a growing link between expert systems and robotics is evident. With present vision systems, the traditional algorithmic approaches are normally used. AI methods, using heuristics, inferential techniques and other devices, may be expected to bring new levels of sophistication to robotic sensor facilities. Johnston (1984) outlines some recent advances in the development of intelligent robots.

There are now commercial expert systems for dozens of different subject areas. In addition to the systems already cited and those described in more detail below, we can mention:

MOLGEN, for the analysis and synthesis of DNA

DART, for diagnosing computer system faults

SPEAR, for analysing computer error logs

SACON, for assisting in structural engineering

AGE, for developing expert systems

LDS, for making legal (product liability) decisions

CALLISTO, for modelling large manufacturing projects

AIRPLAN, for planning military air-traffic movement

HYDRO, for solving water resource problems

WAVES, for advising on seismic data analysis

GENESIS, for planning gene-splicing experiments

CADUCEUS, for medical diagnosis

TATR, for tactical air targeteering

This list, which could easily be extended, shows the range of expert systems currently functioning and under development. There can be little doubt that this trend will continue in the future. As topics such as knowledge representation and the heuristics of effective problem solving are better understood, and as experience of functional expert systems grows, it will be increasingly possible to provide computer-based advisory facilities in any specific subject domain. Wherever human expertise exists it will be possible, in principle, to model this competence in artificial systems. It is not difficult to imagine how the increasing availability of low-cost expert systems will impinge on the professional employment scene. As one consequence, specialists in every field will experience the employment insecurities, caused by increased automation, that factory workers have known for decades.

There is even a suggestion that expert systems may already be more widespread than we think. Thus Alex d'Agapeyeff, principal of Consultants in Information Technology, now Expertech, speaking in December 1984 at a meeting of MPs, civil servants and others organised by Motorola, suggested that companies may be tempted to keep quiet about their own expert systems in order to maintain a competitive advantage. He observed: 'Academics talk about deep skills and uses of expert systems, for example in medicine and other areas, but the ICIs and Unilevers are likely to be using them less for knowledge recording, more for recording empirical knowledge – and at the same time making a tidy profit'. It is pointed out that even rudimentary expert systems can, for example, improve the performance of the average salesman ('. . . developments in this area will remain secret').

If the proliferation of *known* expert systems is significant perhaps the proliferation of *unknown* expert systems is more so. Governments, as well as commercial enterprises, have an interest in maintaining secrecy in certain areas. It may well be that there are already military and government expert systems working in ways we do not suspect. At the same time it is possible to profile expert systems in many other areas. The systems vary in competence from one field to another, but in all areas it is increasingly assumed that AI-related software has a part to play.

MEDICINE

Computers have been used for medical decision making for about twenty years, employing programs that carried out well-established statistical procedures. In the main, the programs focused on the diagnostic element in consultation. Once symptoms had been presented, the computer would select one disease from a fixed set, using methods such as pattern recognition through discriminant functions, Bayesian decision theory, and decision-tree techniques. In more complex programs, *sequential* diagnosis was carried out. This involved specifying a new test for the patient in order to supplement insufficient information for a reliable diagnosis. Here the best test is selected according to economic factors, possible danger to the patient, and the amount of useful information that the test would yield.

By 1980 a wide range of diagnostic systems had been investigated. In one survey (Rogers et al, 1979), a table of 58 empirically tested computer-aided medical systems is presented (see Table 3.1).

In this context, computers are seen as having several inherent capabilities well suited to medical problem-solving:

— the ability to store large quantities of data, without distortion, over long periods of time;

— the ability to recall data exactly as stored;

— the ability to perform complex logical and mathematical operations at high speed;

— the ability to display many diagnostic possibilities in an orderly fashion.

The accuracy of a computer-based diagnostic system depends upon many factors: the depth of the data (knowledge) base, the complexity of the diagnostic task, the selected algorithm, etc. In the Rogers et al (1979) review of applications, it was found that 60 per cent of all the diagnostic studies used an algorithm based on Bayes' theorem. Furthermore, there was a correlation between the disease class and the kind of algorithm used to make the diagnosis. Some computer-based diagnostic systems have performed better than medical consultants, and it is likely that automatic diagnostic systems will be increasingly common in various medical areas. At the same time it is important to recognise the limitations of computer-based medical systems. Moreover, attention will have to be given to the psychological elements in using a computer in the consulting room.

During the 1970s, efforts were made to apply AI techniques to

Disease Type	Number of Studies
Endocrine, nutritional and metabolic	13
Blood and bloodforming organs	2
Mental disorders	10
Nervous system and sense organs	1
Circulatory system	5
Respiratory system	2
Digestive system	12
Genitourinary system	2
Pregnancy, childbirth and the puerperium	1
Skin and subcutaneous tissue	3
Musculoskeletal system, connective tissue	1
Symptoms, ill-defined conditions	4
Accidents, poisonings, violence	2
Total	58

Table 3.1   Number of Articles in Computer-Aided Diagnosis
(See bibliography in Rogers et al, 1979)

problems in medical diagnosis. Again difficulties relating to inexact knowledge were evident: for instance, a particular treatment could not be guaranteed to result in a particular patient state. This situation stimulated the search for methods of representing *inexact knowledge* and for performing *plausible reasoning*. Diagnosis in the medical domain has been depicted as a problem of hypothesis formation, with clinical findings being used to generate a consistent set of disease hypotheses. The various expert systems devoted to medical diagnosis exploit different approaches to the task of hypothesis formation.

There are now many operating expert systems in medicine. Barr and Feigenbaum (1982) highlight typical programs (and also provide full bibliographic citations in each instance).

Attention may be drawn to MYCIN, CASNET, INTERNIST, PIP, the Digitalis Therapy Advisor, IRIS and EXPERT. In addition, there are various experimental programs being developed, including:

—   PUFF, a pulmonary-function program;

—   HODGKINS, a system for performing diagnostic planning for Hodgkins disease;

—   HEADMED, a psychopharmacology advisor;

—   VM, an intensive care monitor;

—   ONCOCIN, a program for monitoring the treatment of oncology out-patients on experimental treatment regimens.

The MYCIN expert system is intended to provide consultative advice on diagnosis and treatment for infectious diseases. This is a useful facility because the attending physician may not be an expert on infectious diseases: for example, an infection may develop after heart surgery, with a consequent need for prompt treatment in conditions of uncertainty. We have already seen that medical knowledge is stored in MYCIN as a set of rules augmented by certainty factors. The factors are used to express the strength of belief in the conclusion of a rule, assuming that all the premises are true.

The MYCIN rules are stored in LISP form and individually

comprise a piece of domain-specific information including an ACTION (often a conclusion) that is justified when the conditions in the PREMISE are fulfilled. Figure 3.2 shows a typical MYCIN rule (this is the LISP form of the rule given in English).

```
PREMISE:        (  AND    (SAME CNTXT INFECT PRIMARY-
                          BACTEREMIA)
                          (MEMBF CNTXT SITE STERILESITES)
                          (SAME CNTXT PORTAL GI)   )
ACTION                    (CONCLUDE CNTXT IDENT BACTERIODES TALLY .7)
```

Figure 3.2   MYCIN Rule 050

Formal evaluations of MYCIN suggest that the system performance compares favourably with that of human experts on such diseases as bacteremia and meningitis. The TEIRESIAS system operates to allow the expert to inspect faulty reasoning chains and to augment and repair MYCIN's medical knowledge. There is a consensus that the MYCIN system shows great promise.

The Causal ASsociational NETwork (CASNET) program was developed at Rutgers University to perform medical diagnosis, with the major application in the field of glaucoma. Here the disease is not represented as a static state but as a dynamic process that can be modelled as a network of causally connected pathophysiological states. The system identifies a discerned pattern of causal pathways with a disease category, whereupon appropriate treatments can be specified. The use of a causal model also facilitates prediction of the development of the disease in a range of treatment circumstances.

CASNET, adopting a strictly bottom-up approach, works from tests, through the causal pathways, to final diagnosis. Though principally applied to glaucoma, the system exhibits a representational scheme and decision-making procedures that are applicable to other diseases. Ophthalmologists have evaluated CASNET and deemed it close to expert level.

The INTERNIST consultation program, developed at the University of Pittsburgh, operates in the domain of internal medicine. A list of disease manifestations (eg symptoms, laboratory data, history, etc) is presented to the system, and diseases that would account for the manifestations are diagnosed. The program then discriminates between competing disease hypotheses. Diagnosis in the field of internal medicine can be difficult because more than one disease may be present in the same patient.

The system's knowledge of diseases is organised in a disease tree, with use made of the *'form-of'* relation (eg hepatocellular disease is a form of liver disease). The top-level classification is by organs – heart disease, lung disease, etc. A list of manifestations, entered at the beginning of a consultation, evokes one or more nodes in the tree (when a model is generated for each evoked node). In this case, a diagnosis corresponds to the set of evoked nodes that account for all the symptoms. INTERNIST-I has been enhanced to form INTERNIST-II (which diagnoses diseases by dividing the disease tree into smaller and smaller subtrees). The system already carries more than 500 of the diseases of internal medicine, ie it is about 75 per cent complete, and practical clinical use is anticipated.

The Present Illness Program (PIP), being developed at MIT, focuses on kidney disease. The system's medical knowledge is represented in frames which centre around diseases, clinical states, and the physiological state of the patient: thirty-six such frames have been constructed to deal with kidney disease. Like INTER-NIST but unlike MYCIN, PIP is designed to simulate the clinical reasoning of physicians.

Other work at MIT, carried out by the Clinical Decision Making Research Group, has been concerned with developing programs to advise physicians on the use of the drug *digitalis*. It is assumed that a patient requires digitalis: the programs determine an appropriate treatment regimen and its subsequent management in these circumstances. This approach is unusual in that it focuses on the problem of continuing patient management. This system, the Digitalis Therapy Advisor, was evaluated by comparing its recommendations to the actual treatments prescribed by human consultants for nineteen patients. On average a panel of experts preferred the recommendations of the physician, but the program's recommendations were reckoned to be the same or better in 60 to 70 per cent of all the cases that were examined.

Another medical system, IRIS, was developed for building, and experimenting with, other consultation systems. The system, designed at Rutgers University and written in INTERLISP, is intended to allow easy experimentation with alternative representations of medical knowledge, clinical strategies, etc. It has assisted in the development of a consultation system for glaucoma.

The EXPERT (expert) system, again developed at Rutgers, is aimed at helping researchers to design and test consultation models. Its development has been influenced by work in building consultation models in such medical areas as rheumatology, ophthalmology and endocrinology. (Experimental models have been developed in other areas, eg chemistry, oil-well log analysis, laboratory-instrument use, and car servicing.)

What we are seeing is a proliferation of expert system programs devoted to (first-order) diagnosis and related tasks, and to the (second-order) development of consultation systems. Whatever the task of a medical expert, it should in principle be amenable to investigation (and subsequent simulation) using expert system methods.

We have noted features of expert systems and indicated how wide-ranging is the work in this area. Attention has already been drawn to systems (ie MECS-AI, ANTICIPATOR and μ-RHEUM) being developed in Japan. Here it is emphasised that all the medical consultation systems are at present in the experimental stage. Some of the research draws on the use of DBMS facilities and detailed medical knowledge. This has recently been highlighted in connection with cancer research (Durham, 1984).

A significant advance was made when the sequence of an oncogene – a cancer gene carried by a virus – was matched with the amino acid pattern of a growth factor present in normal cells. It is suggested that cancer may occur when some normal genes are 'switched on' in error. This discovery was made by a brute-force search of a nucleic-acid/protein database, an approach that is less and less practical as the gene and protein sequences proliferate. A more effective, more intelligent way of identifying matching sequences is required – and this is another reason why increasing attention is being given to AI methods.

In medicine, as elsewhere, expert systems and other AI-related techniques are being developed to tackle diagnostic, research, advisory and other tasks. Most of the medical expert systems are only available on mainframe computers but increasingly the possibilities of micro-based medical systems are being explored. This will have implications for the GP surgery, the domestic environment, etc.

GEOLOGY

Various computer-based systems are being developed to aid geologists engaged in exploration tasks. One of the best known of these systems is PROSPECTOR, being developed at SRI International to help geologists working on problems in hard-rock mineral exploration. (PROSPECTOR made news in 1982 when it was given the same field study data about a region in Washington State as that used by experts in a mining company. The system concluded that there were deposits of molybdenum over a wide area. The geologists disagreed but when exploratory drilling was undertaken PROSPECTOR was found to be right.)

The user provides PROSPECTOR with information about a region (eg data on rock types, minerals, alteration products, etc), whereupon the program matches the information against its models. Where necessary, PROSPECTOR asks the user for more information to enable a decision to be reached. The user can intervene at any stage to provide new data, change existing information or request an evaluation from the system. A sophisticated inference network is used to control PROSPECTOR's reasoning, with network nodes corresponding to various geological assertions (eg *There is alteration favourable for the potassic zone of a porphyry copper deposit*). Rules are employed to specify how the probability of one assertion affects the probability of another (these inference rules are analogous to the production rules used in MYCIN).

A geologist using PROSPECTOR prepares a model as an inference network. The current system contains five different models (developed in cooperation with five consulting geologists): Koroko-type massive sulphide, Mississippi-Valley-type lead/zinc, type A porphyry copper, Komatiitic nickel sulphide, and roll-front sandstone uranium. These models are collectively represented by 541 assertions and 327 rules. Using the models and input data, the system is able to adjust the probability of hypotheses in changing circumstances.

The five models have only recently been developed to the point when useful geological evaluations could be made. And many further models are needed for extensive coverage of the full prospecting domain.

In another application of AI-related methods of geological surveying, the UK company, Oilfield Expert Systems Ltd, has developed a knowledge-based modelling system to aid oilfield analysis. This facility, called the Integrated Knowledge-Based Modelling System (IKBM), provides a rapid-prototyping method for developing expert systems. A model of the oilfield is constructed from the user's data, and specialists from various disciplines are asked to feed in their own data. The system then integrates the data into its own model, combining the new information into selected interpretations. The resulting model, which runs on a Symbolics 3600 Lisp machine, can be tested and modified in on-line working.

CHEMISTRY

Expert systems are now finding applications in many areas of scientific research and investigation: for example, in chemical analysis, geological prospecting, and the solution of mathematical problems in engineering and physics. Computer programs have been widely applied in all the sciences for many years, but specifically AI methods have had a more limited application. In, for example, non-numeric chemical reasoning problems, these methods have been applied to:

— identifying molecular structures in unknown organic compounds;

— planning a sequence of reactions to synthesise organic chemical compounds.

The identification of molecular structures is important to a wide range of problems in chemistry, biology and medicine. In many cases, the sophisticated analytic methods of x-ray crystallography may not be practical, and researchers must interpret data obtained in other ways, eg via mass spectrometry. Some tests allow the chemist to discover *molecular fragments,* subparts of the molecule, from which characteristic *constraints* can be derived. These constraints are interpreted as graph features in the representation of the molecule. Some of the current AI programs use similar data to generate small subsets of the theoretically-possible structures. The identification of molecular structures, using this type of approach, is being tackled by such expert systems as DENDRAL, CONGEN, Meta-DENDRAL and CRYSALIS. By contrast, such expert systems as LHASA, SECS and SYNCHEM are concerned with finding techniques for the laboratory synthesis of known substances.

The (Heuristic) DENDRAL program, following the formulation of the DENDRAL algorithm in 1964, identifies the possible molecular structures of constituent atoms that could account for the given spectroscopic analysis of the molecule under investigation. One main purpose of the heuristic approach was to replace the exhaustive method of the algorithm by a more economical strategy. The program achieved the objective by supplementing the DENDRAL algorithm with rules derived from expert chemists using mass spectrographic data. However, the chemists had difficulty in explicating their expertise, and the Meta-DENDRAL project was launched in 1970 to develop a means of inferring the rules of mass spectrometry from examples of molecular structures that had already been successfully analysed by human experts.

By the mid-1970s it was found that limitations on the DENDRAL algorithm allowed Heuristic DENDRAL to generate only acyclic structures (ie ketones, alcohols, ethers, amines, etc). In 1976 the CONGEN program was designed to function without the acyclic limitation.

The Heuristic DENDRAL project – from its late-1960s inception to the present – has yielded various significant results. Though the system knows far less than a human expert, it elucidates structures efficiently by searching through possibilities. Published papers (cited in Barr and Feigenbaum, 1982) have variously shown that the program can solve structure elucidation problems for complex organic molecules, and that – for example, in the analysis of mass spectra of mixtures of oestrogenic steroids – the program can perform better than human experts. DENDRAL programs have been employed to determine the structures of various types of molecules (eg terpeniod natural products, marine sterols, chemical impurities, antibiotics, insect pheromones, etc). CONGEN, deriving from the DENDRAL project, is in practical use by chemists to solve various types of problems in the elucidation of molecular structures.

Meta-DENDRAL, designed to infer the rules of mass spectrometry from known structures, learns by scanning hundreds of molecular structure/spectral data-point pairs and by searching the space of fragmentation rules for likely explanations. The rule set can be extended to accommodate new data. The proficiency of Meta-DENDRAL can be estimated in part by the ability of a DENDRAL program using derived rules to predict spectra of new molecules. In fact the program has rediscovered known rules of mass spectrometry for two classes of molecules; and, more importantly, it has discovered *new* rules for three closely-related families of structures (the mono-, di-, and tri-keto androstanes).

The CRYSALIS expert system focuses on protein crystallography, aiming to integrate various sources of knowledge to match the crystallographer's performance in electron-density-map interpretation. (This would fill an important gap in the automation of protein crystallography.) The concept of an electron density map generally denotes some pictorial representation (eg a three-dimensional contour map) of electron density over a certain region. The skilled crystallographer can study such a map to discover features allowing him to infer atomic sites, molecular boundaries, the polymer backbone, etc. In due course a structural model can be built to conform to the electron density map. Automation of this task requires a computational system that could generate, display and test hypotheses.

In CRYSALIS the hypotheses are represented in a hierarchical data structure, with knowledge sources able to add, change and test hypothesis elements on a 'blackboard' (see Knowledge Representation, above). The system can at present only perform a portion of the total task of interpreting electron density maps. The knowledge base is relatively small, but this is expanding and a capability is envisaged for the complete interpretation of medium-quality medium-resolution electron density maps.

We have already mentioned the three major organic synthesis programs. LHASA (Logic and Heuristics Applied to Synthetic Analysis), maintained at Harvard, is the earliest. This system yielded SECS (Simulation and Evaluation of Chemical Synthesis), now being developed at the University of California. SECS extended the LHASA approach by more extensively exploiting stereochemical and other types of information. The third major program of this sort. SYNCHEM (SYNthetic CHEMistry), is being developed at the State University of New York.

The main item of knowledge in chemical synthesis is the chemical reaction. Here a rule describes a) a situation in which a molecular structure can be changed, and b) the change itself. The programs use knowledge of reactions to design a synthesis route from starting materials to target molecule. In summary:

— the LHASA knowledge base, a set of procedures, contains very sophisticated chemistry knowledge but is difficult to update;

— the SECS knowledge base, carrying about 400 separate transforms, allows new transforms to be added without the need for program changes;

— the SYNCHEM knowledge base includes a library of reactions and commercially-available starting compounds. Chemists can modify the knowledge base without reprogramming.

Computer-aided chemical synthesis is regarded as a potentially valuable new facility for chemists, whether engaged in research or industrial manufacturing. A key factor in expert systems devoted to organic synthesis is how much they know about chemical reactions. The three main synthesis programs have all demonstrated their ability to find synthetic routes for organic materials.

In one practical application, ICI is offering an AI-related service to British farmers. Wheat Counsellor, the first expert system to be available through videotex, uses a knowledge base held on a central computer. Videotex terminals, located in ICI's agrochemical distributor's offices and showrooms, can be used to access the knowledge. When information is fed in about variety of wheat being grown, soil conditions, crop history, local weather conditions and disease patterns, Wheat Counsellor can make recommendations for controlling diseases in winter wheat. The system suggests treatments using both ICI's own chemicals and products from other manufacturers, analyses costs, predicts likely returns on investment, and offers advice on a field-by-field basis. Wheat Counsellor is reckoned to be the only farmers' advice system based on expert systems and available through videotex. And just as diseases in foodstuffs can be controlled using AI-related software, so environmental chemicals can be screened by expert systems for their possible danger to human beings. Thus Gottinger (1984) describes the design of Hazard, an expert system for screening environmental chemicals on carcinogenicity.

The aims of Hazard are to monitor a potentially hazardous waste facility, to detect deviations from normal operating conditions, to evaluate the situation, and to recommend appropriate action. To perform these tasks it operates on a large chemical knowledge base using an inference engine. The structure of Hazard is similar to that of Mycin, though it functions at a deeper level (ie it is said to be a second-generation expert-system (ES) technology (EST) system). Hazard can be transplanted to other diagnostic-testing settings (such as drug monitoring, regulation of food additives, etc), and is intended to be fully domain independent.

The use of (first- and second-generation) expert systems for chemical research and the surveillance of chemical products is an immensely complex field. As with medicine, research into the use of AI-related techniques in pure and applied chemistry is proceeding simultaneously on many different fronts.

MATHEMATICS

MACSYMA, originally designed in 1968, is a large computer system used to assist mathematicians, scientists and engineers in tackling mathematical problems. It accepts symbolic inputs and yields symbolic outputs, and, in addition to its algebraic-manipulation competence, it includes a large numerical subroutine library. Today MACSYMA, running on a DEC KL-10 at MIT and accessed through the ARPA Network, is used by hundreds of US researchers. Many workers from government laboratories, universities and private companies spend much of every day logged in to the system.

As with many other expert systems, the performance of MACSYMA relies upon an extensive knowledge base. This enables the interactive system to perform more than 600 different types of mathematical operations, including differentiation, integration, equation solving, matrix operations, and vector algebra. MACSYMA currently comprises about 230,000 words of compiled LISP code and a similar amount of code written in the special MACSYMA programming language.

Many of the system algorithms were known before the development of MACSYMA, while others evolved during the system research. AI helped to frame the environment in which MACSYMA was born, and various AI-related capabilities are currently being developed in the system (for example, a new representation for algebraic expressions and a knowledge-based 'apprentice').

MACSYMA has many powerful capabilities. A handout issued by Symbolics Inc indicates why users can achieve greater productivity:

— They can explore extremely complex problems that cannot be solved in any other manner;

— They have access to mathematical techniques that are not available from any other computing resources;

— The results obtained are exact. Since they can be checked by independent procedures, costly error analysis is eliminated;

— The system can generate FORTRAN expressions automatically. This reduces the element of human error and speeds development of accurate code;

— The system offers a new plateau of computing power and versatility, allowing users to concentrate on the intellectual content of a problem. This often provides a user with insight into the fundamental nature of the problem itself;

— The system can be used as an advanced calculator to perform everyday symbolic and numerical problems.

The prodigious range of this system is particularly impressive. Application areas include such fields as:

— acoustics;

— algebraic geometry;

— computer-aided design;

— control theory;

— decision analysis in clinical medicine;

— economics;

— fluid mechanics;

— number theory;

— numerical analysis;

— plasma physics;

— structural mechanics;

— solid-state physics.

Countless problems have been explored in these various fields. For example, there have been studies in antenna theory, atomic scattering, ballistic missile systems, emulsion chemistry, LSI circuit design, helicopter blade motion, ship hull design, and underwater shock waves. MACSYMA, employing a prodigious diversity of algorithmic and heuristic techniques, is one of the most powerful mathematical systems in the world. It is now available for licensing on various computer systems (eg the Symbolics LM-2 and 3600, the DEC VAX and 20 series, and the Honeywell Multics systems).

Professor Stanly Steinberg (Department of Mathematics, University of New Mexico) has used MACSYMA to generate Fortran subroutines used in the simulation of lasers. He has declared that MACSYMA 'can do computations that are impossible to do by hand' and that the system packs 'certainly more than a lifetime's worth of work' into a manageable amount of computer time (quoted by Ritter, 1984). In one case, Dr Richard Pavelle (of

Symbolics) saw a calculation (that had taken three months by hand) redone by MACSYMA in two minutes. Symbolics has now licensed the system to 250 sites worldwide.

Another mathematical program is AM, described as a system that 'models one aspect of mathematical research, modelling new concepts'. However, AM's claims are contentious. Researchers at Heriot Watt University in Edinburgh have criticised AM's ability to discover new mathematical concepts. In any event it is clear that mathematical expert systems are offering invaluable services to industry, science, government and education. Computer-based algebraic systems have various advantages. Pavelle and colleagues have summarised (in *Scientific American,* December 1981) some of the benefits of algebraic systems:

— some concepts in science (eg pi) are better left as symbols rather than turned into a number, because in that way round-off errors can be avoided. Errors can accumulate with successive operations, requiring careful error analysis;

— computer time can be saved if a mathematical expression is simplified algebraically before it is evaluated numerically. This reduction can reach a factor of 100 or more;

— an algebraic approach may give the researcher insights into the problem, which may not otherwise have been obtained.

It has been emphasised that a computer-based algebraic system can be more useful than a human mathematician. Pavelle has pointed out that MACSYMA solves differential equations almost at human-expert level, can perform integrals beyond the capacities of human beings, and in due course will surpass all human abilities in both speed and capability.

PROCESS CONTROL

Picon, an expert system from Lisp Machines Inc, assists industrial process control operators in complex plants where only a few people are needed to regulate hundreds of highly automated processes. The system operates in real time, collecting data from (up to 20,000) sensors and alarms. It can cope with a flood of data that would swamp even the most competent human operators.

The system is initially instructed in the details of a particular process application, with users then led through the process using an interactive, graphics-oriented display. The users enter system operation parameters, critical variables and other details of expert operator knowledge. At this stage, an expert computer model of the plant processes has been constructed, whereupon Picon can be put into operation.

Picon runs on a Lambda/Plus dedicated Lisp machine that has two processors: a Lisp processor that handles the 'expertise' side of the operation, and a 68010 processor which handles calculations, monitors sensors and alarms, and feeds information to the Lisp processor. The system, once installed, can continue to learn. Picon can explain its recommendations if the operators disagree, and further knowledge can be incorporated to improve future decision making. The addition of new knowledge is a straightforward matter: the operator simply calls up the knowledge-capture interface used to build the original model, and then supplies the new information.

ENGINEERING DIAGNOSTICS

The computer retrieval incidence bank (CRIB) is one of several expert systems designed for computer fault diagnosis (see description in Hartley, 1984). The system can be used for diagnosis of faults in both hardware and software, and relies upon a knowledge base of simple factual information that can support the diagnostic task. The system designers investigated 1) the knowledge required by an engineer to find faults, and 2) how this knowledge is used by a skilled human practitioner. CRIB, now comprising a configuration of four programs, is regarded by its designers as a prototype for better systems. Another fault diagnosis system, FALOSY (FAult LOcalisation SYstem, described by Sedlmeyer et al, 1983) is used specifically for program debugging. More ambitiously, the New Medius expert system, from IAL Data Communications, is intended to locate network faults and (when system development is complete) to fix them by organising repairs.

The task of fault diagnosis requires the application of a set of techniques to a particular subject domain. It is easy to envisage a general fault-diagnosis system that can be bolted on to different knowledge bases. However, most research into expert-system fault diagnosis has focused on particular subject areas: computer circuits, electrical wiring, network connections, etc. Pratt (1984) describes a computerised diagnostic system using AI techniques plus the expertise of an engineer to diagnose faults in locomotives. The system, developed by the General Electric Company's New York Corporate Research and Development Centre, will soon be widely used in railroad service depots throughout the United States. A central aim is to give the system humanlike modes of reasoning.

A project at Bath University has used the Sage expert system shell to build an expert system for fault diagnosis for a furniture manufacturer. And in yet another application area, General Motors is aiming to exploit AI techniques to help motor mechanics to diagnose faults in cars. (General Motors has paid $3 million for an 11 per cent interest in the Californian artificial intelligence firm, Teknowledge.) Faults in computer circuits can be uncovered using a similar approach. The DART expert system, for example, already mentioned, can locate specific hardware and software components likely to be responsible for an observed fault. The system can also give reasons for its conclusions, pointing to the major factors and relevant evidence that are used in analysing the problem.

COMPUTER-AIDED DESIGN

There is increasing scope for expert systems in a wide range of design applications. One aim is to 'pit knowledge against complexity, using expert knowledge to whittle complexity down to a manageable scale' (Stefik and de Kleer, 1983). In this way, expert systems can be used in, for example, digital system design, one of many possibilities being researched at Digital Equipment Corporation (DEC) and elsewhere. With one experimental expert system, transistor size in integrated circuits is determined and circuit parameters such as load and capacitance are defined. In 1978 DEC began work, in conjunction with Carnegie-Mellon University, to develop a knowledge-based program called XCON for configuring VAX-11/780 computers. EURISTO, an AI program used to configure naval fleets in competition games, has recently been employed to search for useful microcircuits structures made possible by multilayer fabrication technology.

At the Massachusetts Institute of Technology the Artificial Intelligence Laboratory has been experimenting with expert systems for many years. Systems such as EL and SYN help designers to analyse and synthesise analogue circuits. The PALLADIO system, developed at Xerox and Stanford University, is intended to help designers to experiment with new methodologies. A designer can discover gaps in the knowledge base by applying it to his own design, allowing subsequent modifications (to both knowledge base and design) to be made.

Thomas et al (1983) describe how expert-system methods are now being applied to the synthesis and design of VLSI circuits for computers and other systems. Emphasis is given to the development of the CMU-DA system which uses a behavioural statement to propose functional block components and alternate block inter-connections that will implement the specified behaviour. A computer-aided design environment is being developed to aid the automatic synthesis of the behavioural and functional block levels of design. Here programs such as DAA and EMUCS are used for synthesis purposes. Using another approach, an expert system called SMX-Cogitor has been developed in Sweden to perform structural analysis and to check programs and problem solutions.

Expert systems can be seen to have various advantages over conventional computer-aided design (CAD) techniques. For example, symbolic languages facilitate the representation of design concepts; the expert-systems approach makes it easier to cope with uncertainty; and a knowledge base makes it easier to represent (often informal and heuristic) design expertise. These advantages have encouraged computer manufacturers to develop systems to aid in the configuring of computer designs to meet customer requirements. Thus IBM and NCR are developing configuring systems, and ICL has developed the Dragon sizing system to help sales engineers to estimate a customer's workload requirements and the computer system needed to match them. Similarly companies such as Xerox, Fairchild, Hewlett Packard and Daisy Systems are using expert systems to aid VLSI design. XCON, mentioned above, is one of the best known expert systems used for configuring computer systems.

The XCON facility, developed by DEC, now runs on machines in the US and England to configure VAX systems. It is being extended to cover PDP models as well. Dennis O'Connor, the manager responsible for the system, has commented that XCON 'has become part of the way DEC does business'. The system provides output according to the specific order from a customer. For example, an order for a VAX 780 with a 456M byte disk drive, Ethernet access link and other options will cause XCON to give details on:

— components needed to complete the configuration, plus explanation;

— components ordered but not immediately required;

— a layout for the proposed computer room;

— layouts of components in cabinets, and locations of connections;

— unibus length and load, and box power requirement;

— unused capacity in the system;

— cables required and points connected;

— required settings of address and vector switches.

The flexibility of the DEC approach is seen as essential to the company's competitive position.

The increasing use of expert systems for engineering design has implications not only for commercial activity – we would expect customers to respond well to DEC's 'tailor-made' approach – but also for the role of professional designers. It is not difficult to see how staffing requirements might diminish in the future, though at present AI techniques are supplementing, rather than supplanting, human enterprise. The growing prevalence of expert systems in a CAD environment is reflected in the literature: systems are profiled and techniques are explored (see, for example, Simmons, 1984) – and some of the work described in the journals derives from specific funded projects, such as the Japanese fifth-generation initiative.

One of the first practical applications of Japanese AI research has been announced by Nippon Electric (NEC). This company has designed a CAD facility, including an expert system, for chip design. The system is easy to use, and it cuts design time very dramatically. Use is made of Prolog, popular as an AI language, and Fortran, long employed in CAD applications. Other design facilities, using AI-related techniques, are planned.

The move towards implementing expert systems for design purposes has an obvious market relevance. Products can be more accurately directed at customer needs and successes in one design area lead to useful initiatives in another. DEC, for instance, is integrating various expert systems and is launching related AI systems of other types: for example, a fault finder (AI-Spear) and a training system (TeachVMS). Expert systems for design often work in conjunction with other AI facilities intended for other purposes.

BUSINESS AND FINANCE

Expert systems will become increasingly available to business and office workers, just as they will emerge in the factory and engineering environments. For example, the Financial Advisor (based on the Nexus expert system) has been launched by Helix Products and Marketing as an aid for businessmen and other professional people. Financial Advisor offers advice on business management and helps to diagnose financial problems. Other Helix systems are Investment Advisor (to analyse investment possibilities) and Car Advisor (for those people deciding how to buy a car and which one), with other areas – such as personnel, loan administration, tax policies, etc – already targeted for expert-system development.

TAXADVISOR is an expert system (described by Michaelsen and Michie, 1983) designed to make tax planning recommendations for businessmen and other users. The system asks questions about a client's current wealth, and then gives advice to help him maximise his wealth within certain constraints. Another system, AUDITOR, developed at the University of Illinois, has been developed to help auditors assess a company's allowance for bad debts. Auditing information was assembled in rule form, initially for use on the AL/X system developed at the University of Edinburgh. Other systems are TAXMAN (for evaluating the tax consequences of certain types of proposed business reorganisation) and CORPTAX (to advise the user about redemption policies).

A wide range of expert systems are being developed by DEC for in-house use. These include XSITE (an expert site planner's assistant), IMACS (to aid manufacturing), ISA (to aid scheduling), IPMS (to aid project management), XPRESS (to aid the refining of organisational procedures) and ILRPS (to aid long-range planning). XSEL, designed to help the salesperson develop system orders, was introduced for use in the US in September 1983 with the aim of extending its usage worldwide in 1984/5. This system interfaces between sales and engineering, addresses the problems of incorrect sales configuration, unprepared sites and unrealistic delivery estimates. DEC, with 22 departments working on AI projects, aims to encourage development of both commercial and in-house expert systems.

In a telecommunications development relevant to the office worker, Xionics has introduced the Isolink modules to allow non-technical users of the Xibus multifunction workstation to access computer systems, databanks, networks and other facilities. This type of development will be influenced by progress in expert systems. And marketing also will be affected by the emergence of AI-related products.

Persoft Inc (in Woburn, Mass) has introduced an expert system to help direct marketing organisations. Users are given guidance about which listed names should be excluded from promotions. Thus the Mail Order Response Enhancer (More) analyses historical response data or the results of a test mailing and identifies the characteristics of a likely respondent. Then the package assigns a statistical response value to each name on a list, from most likely to respond to least likely. The raw data is input, whereupon the entire file is automatically matched against the test data.

The More package progressively incorporates new data into its forecasting equation. Hence the system can *learn* from one mailing to the next, continually refining its profile of a likely respondent. In addition, More can use the client's mailing lists to target entire groups of people who may be likely to respond to new products. The package is priced at $375,000 (early-1985).

As with other application areas, increasing attention is being given to how expert systems can be used in sales, marketing and financial services. Various start-up companies are focusing their efforts solely on these product areas. For example, Applied Expert Systems (Apex), Inference Corporation and Syntelligence are targeting financial services as a major application field. In this context specific applications have been identified as, for example, credit extension, financial planning, foreign exchange operations, insurance underwriting, and asset and liability management. Folio, developed by Paul Cohen (Stanford) and Mark Lieberman (Drexel Burnham Lambert) is one successful expert system in this field.

Folio uses a 50-rule, forward-chaining knowledge-based system to generate an automatic assessment of a client's investment goals. A simple interview system allows client data to be gathered, and a linear programming algorithm optimises the distribution of assets between nine different fund types once the goals have been determined. The main contribution of Folio is to identify the most suitable investment goals. In a similar way, banks can be helped to explore alternative financial strategies. Inference Corporation has suggested that an expert system for this purpose could be based on its ART expert-system shell. The aim would be to suggest alternative strategies and the reasoning behind them.

Financial AI-related applications are required to meet a number of specific criteria. For example, Sandra Cook, manager of financial expert systems at SRI International (California), proposed at a late-1984 seminar that a financial problem is amenable to an expert-system treatment in particular circumstances:

— where no adequate algorithmic solution exists;

— where a poor decision will have serious cost consequences;

— where it is likely that a non-expert will make a poor decision (the machine should be superior);

— where the problem allows the machine sufficient time for analysis (ie the problem is relatively static);

— where the problem can be solved by an expert;

— where the knowledge domain, like the problem, is relatively static;

— where the political climate is friendly to the new technology.

For such circumstances to obtain, it is essential that financial applications be chosen with care.

LAW AND ADMINISTRATION

Computer-based facilities are commonplace in these areas, though AI systems are relative newcomers. Already so-called expert systems are helping lawyers – for example, to search for legal precedents in various comprehensive databases. But not all such systems embody AI-related techniques: instead they rely on traditional search and retrieval methods. Examples of computer-based facilities in this area include:

— the Legol language, used to express legal concepts;

— the LRS system, used to perform knowledge-based legal information retrieval;

— the DSCAS system that analyses differing site condition claims in the area of contract management.

Waterman and Peterson (1984) describe the LDS rule-based scheme for representing legal expertise revealed in systematic interviews. Future work is expected to focus on case features that affect the settlement strategy, how litigators process information (how do they deal with uncertainty?), differences among litigators, and the process of negotiation and settlement.

Administrative expert systems may also be required to settle payment claims: for example, the UK Department of Health and Social Security intends to use expert systems in its social security offices – members of the public will be informed about the payments to which they are entitled and how to obtain them. In another application, a team at Imperial College (London) is developing an expert system to interpret the British Nationality Act. The system was originally devised for an IBM Personal Computer as an exercise in bringing together the logical analysis of legislation and the computerisation of logic. Text from the Act has been embedded in APES (A Prolog Expert System Shell) and can be used for the generation of explanations. The system can also interrogate the user to elicit information not contained in the knowledge base. An academic paper discussing APES comments: 'the experience gained in managing large and complex bodies of legislation may have important lessons for the engineering of large and complex software. We believe the formalisation of legislation is a fruitful domain not only for artificial intelligence technology but also for software engineering'.

In a more mundane role, expert systems can simply aid the retrieval process (expert systems have in fact been characterised as mere extensions to traditional information retrieval methods). Hence American Metals Climax Inc is using the AI-based J-Space document indexing-and-retrieval system: around 600 employees can quickly find any desired item among more than 5000 long proprietary documents stored on a DECsystem 20. J-Space can also run on the Alpha Micro microcomputer. Sophisticated searching, using AI techniques, can aid many administrative tasks.

TELECOMMUNICATIONS

We have seen (for example, Narendra and Mars, 1983) how learning algorithms can be used in telephone traffic routeing. Today learning and other artificial-intelligent activities are increasingly evident in telecommunications. Jones and Watson (1984) list potential applications for expert systems in this area:

—   intelligent electronic mail systems which could learn from errors and take initiatives in communicating with users;

—   consultant for system configuration that could be used as a design tool or consultant by the telecommunications manager;

—   expert maintenance system that would respond as would a skilled engineer to specific faults;

—   expert control system that would provide current status reports, procedural changes and breakdown diagnoses.

In this context, software may be expected to become more user friendly: Business Information Techniques Ltd has coined the phrase 'helpful software' to denote improved ergonomics, enhanced user interfaces, expert systems and natural-language support.

EDUCATION

Computer technology has been applied to education since the early-1960s, with applications in such areas as course-scheduling, test-grading, and the management of teaching aids. One aim of CAI (Computer-Aided Instruction) research has been to build instructional programs that incorporate course material in lessons that are optimised for each student. In the Intelligent CAI (ICAI) programs that began to emerge in the 1970s, course material was conveyed independently of teaching procedures – to enable problems and comments to be generated differently for each student. Today, AI is influencing the design of programs that are sensitive to the student's strengths and weaknesses, and to the preferred style of learning.

Early research on ICAI systems tended to concentrate on the representation of the subject matter. Attention may be drawn to such benchmark efforts as: SCHOLAR, a geography tutor; SOPHIE, an electronics troubleshooting tutor; and EXCHECK, a logic and set theory tutor. These systems have a high level of domain expertise, which allows them to be responsive over a wide spectrum of interactive problem-solving situations. Other expert educational programs are:

— WHY, which tutors students in the causes of rainfall, a complex geographical process that is a function of many variables. This system exploits 'socratic tutoring heuristics' and is able to identify and correct student misconceptions. WHY began as an extension of SCHOLAR;

— WEST, described as a program for 'guided discovery' learning. The system, deriving from a board game, assumes that a student *constructs* an understanding of a situation or a task, the notion of progressively corrected misconceptions being central to this assumption. The learning student interacts with a 'Coach';

— WUMPUS, which again uses game techniques to teach a mixture of logic, probability, decision theory and geometry. In one version, the coach is WUSOR-II, a system that involves the interaction of various specialist programs. Four basic modules are used: Expert, Psychologist, Student

Model, and Tutor. The system is recognised to be a useful learning aid;

— GUIDON, a program for diagnostic problem-solving which uses the rules of the MYCIN consultation system. A student engages in a dialogue about a patient suspected of having an infection, and learns how to use clinical and laboratory data for diagnosis purposes. This system goes beyond responding to the student's last move (as in WEST and WUMPUS) and repetitive questioning and answering (as in SCHOLAR and WHY);

— BUGGY, designed to identify a student's basic arithmetic misconceptions. The system can provide an explanation of why a student is making an arithmetic mistake. Experience has indicated that forming a model of what is wrong can be more difficult than performing the task itself. BUGGY can be used to train teachers to diagnose errors in the way that students work.

The above programs are essentially *teaching* systems, and other programs are available to assist *learning by doing*. Emphasis may be given to effective 'learning environments' such as LISP-based LOGO (and its most celebrated application, turtle geometry), the message-passing SMALLTALK (and its extension, THING-LAB), and the DIRECTOR animation system. Here powerful programming-language features are used with sophisticated graphics facilities. AI has contributed to expert systems in the educational environment, as elsewhere.

Current research includes a project at Sussex University, England: Aaron Sloman and T. Pateman have been awarded a grant of £20,000 for a project entitled 'An Expert System to Help Trainee Teachers'.

MILITARY APPLICATIONS

A wide range of military expert-systems applications are being developed (we have already mentioned AIRPLAN, for planning military air-traffic movement, and TATR, for tactical air targeteering). Some systems are intended to introduce AI techniques into war gaming, others to optimise the performance of battlefield weapons. KNOBS, for instance, was one of the first expert systems applied productively to military problems (in this case to interactive planning).

MICROCOMPUTER SELECTION, PERFORMANCE

Already expert systems are fulfilling many different roles in the field of computing itself. We have seen examples of system design (where, for example, products can be configured to a customer's requirements) and diagnosis of faults in electronic circuits. Expert systems are also being used to select computers for particular purposes. Duffin and Lello (1984) describe MASES (Microcomputer Advice and Selection Expert System) which runs on a CP/M microcomputer and incorporates expertise derived from the Central Computer and Telecommunications Agency (CCTA).

The development of MASES followed work using the Isis Micro Expert package to devise a small expert system to diagnose faults on a local area computer network. The aim was for MASES to advise on selection of a microcomputer for a given application from the CCTA's Standard Range. The system asks the user to supply details of the application (information about software, printers, interfaces, etc), whereupon a recommendation is made. MASES has the characteristic expert-systems features of being able to explain its reasoning to a non-expert user.

An expert system able to provide quantitative measurement of the performance of computer software and information systems is to be the first project of an AI research centre established in New South Wales, Australia, in early-1985. This system, to be developed at the Software Productivity Research Centre, will be known as Spacer (Systems Productivity Audit, Comparative Evaluation and Review) and will serve as a key business tool. Scott (1984) briefly outlines the phases of the project.

SUMMARY

This chapter has profiled the various current expert-systems applications areas. The systems vary widely in cost, complexity and competence: most require mainframes or minis (eg VAX) but a few can run on microcomputers. No effort has been made to evaluate the expert systems that are mentioned, and it is likely that a few may be open to the criticism that they do not embody AI techniques proper but simply exploit traditional computing methods. The seeming proliferation of expert systems should not be taken to imply that they are all, in fact, instances of artificial intelligence.

Some characteristics of expert systems have been indicated but few details have been given. It is worth exploring some of the important features of expert systems before indicating companies and products in the microcomputer sector. Some of these features show the reasons why it is difficult to implement fully-fledged expert systems on small machines.

4 Features of Expert Systems

INTRODUCTION

Expert systems have many features that are typical of traditional software but also have unique and characteristic properties. Some sceptics doubt the innovative claims of the expert systems suppliers, at the same time pointing out the heavy demands that expert systems make on processing time and storage capacity. Expert systems, we find, are innovative and revolutionary; or they are pretentious and inefficient. It is likely that such a dichotomy of interpretation is a temporary affair: expert systems will stand or fall in the marketplace – and in any event one half of the argument will wither away.

This chapter highlights some of the characteristic features of expert systems. No attempt is made to give exhaustive definitions, examples of coding, or guidance on writing expert-systems software (though relevant texts are cited, where appropriate). The aim is to convey the *flavour* of expert systems, to draw attention to the sorts of topics that interest system designers and suppliers, to chart the conceptual framework within which functional systems are produced and within which the debate is conducted.

We can see that many of the characteristic features of expert systems bear directly on the implementation of suitable software on microcomputers. If, for example, Lisp or Prolog are deemed to be the most suitable expert-systems languages then micros that cannot cope with Lisp or Prolog dialects may be very limited in their capacity to cope with expert-systems software. Similarly, expert-systems that demand speedy processing are quite unsuited to micros with long cycle times. It is important to appreciate how the characteristic features of expert systems are suited (or not) to implementation on small computer configurations.

COMPUTERS, BRAINS AND MINDS

Much of the AI controversy focuses on analogies, often superficially drawn, between computer behaviour and mental performance. For example, do computers simply *mimic* human mental processes or do they in some sense *duplicate* them? Are the activities in computer CPUs an effective metaphor of human thought or do computers actually think? Such questions have a more than merely semantic significance: they condition to a large extent our expectations of many types of sophisticated computer software. If we do not baulk at the idea that computers can reflect, reason, learn and pay attention we are more likely to be audacious in our efforts to design truly intelligent systems. This does not mean, of course, that we will be successful – only that we stand a better chance than if we are constrained by the less imaginative, traditional categories. This question has been thrown into sharp relief by the burgeoning world of expert systems.

One approach to the possibility of thinking machines is to compare parts of a computer with parts of the human brain. The simplest analogy is the functional resemblance of the brain to a CPU (or a collocation of CPUs) – as when a microprocessor is said to be the 'brain' of a microcomputer. Some neurologists have found what they deem to be columns of 'microprocessors' in the cerebral cortex and in other areas of the central nervous system. In such an interpretation, the brain of man and the higher mammals is a parallel configuration of micros, using neuron impulses and associated chemotransmitters to exploit a binary logic for the purposes of intelligent behaviour. Nature, not the Japanese, first thought of fifth- (and sixth-) generation systems!

It has been pointed out that much of the brain's processing takes place in association with short-term memory which – though having only a limited storage capacity – can quickly change its contents as attention switches from one concern to another. The *hippocampus* – one in each hemisphere of the brain – is specialised for a wide range of logical sequences and operations. It is here that information sets are compared for similarities and differences: use is made of the database of experience to channel information to appropriate processing centres. For instance, the hippocampus can cope with *novelty* (which may demand rapid processing for purposes of biological survival) and *habituation* (where familiar patterns do not need the types of processing to which they have been subject many times before). It is easy to speculate on how a computer system could function in an analogous way, performing discriminations on incoming data and carrying out subsequent tasks according to the results.

An example of such a computer-based approach is Douglas Lenat's program designed to generate mathematical concepts. Here certain primitive concepts are built into the system: for example, the system has an interest in sets of information that satisfy various criteria (eg to determine novelty and habituation). Thus information is sorted and compared with stored information to determine what processing action is necessary. In such a way a computer can mimic well-defined processes occurring in the brain (see also Chapter 3 in Simons, 1984).

Most of the computer-based efforts to mimic brain functions are *cognitive* in character, ie they are concerned with such tasks as remembering, learning, perceiving, problem solving, etc. There are rarely any attempts to mimic *conative* functions, ie tasks associated with willing and desiring. Where, for example, an analogue to *emotion* has been required in a computer system, the programmer has resorted to 'weighting factors' – particular variables have been assigned numbers in order to give them different importances, different values. The emergence of such a rudimentary 'value system' is akin to how parameters can be weighted in a fuzzy-logic treatment of expert systems. Here, in an effort to handle uncertainty, parameters are assigned numbers to allow the possibility of intermediate states between the two binary poles. This is conceptually different from efforts to represent emotion in artefacts but there are interesting procedural similarities.

At a primitive level it is easy to point to cognitive equivalences between brain behaviour and computer performance. In both cases information is stored for future use involving a spectrum of retrieval and processing activities. But such a generalisation disguises a host of problems: for example, how specifically are concepts and values stored in the brain and subsequently exploited to inform judgement and discrimination, and how are analogous features to be built into computer software? Expert systems are supposed to discriminate between options and to assign probability values to conclusions, but at present they can only accomplish such tasks within a limited set of domains (the impressively broad spectrum of applications shown in Chapter 3 disguises the wide variation of competence in operational expert systems). It is one of the contributions of the so-called 'declarative' languages, such as Prolog, that they can be used to describe the relationships between data. It is possible to define the rules needed to solve a problem. This is strictly analogous to how a trained expert is equipped, by building up and storing appropriate routines, to tackle problems in a particular field.

Most of the computer-based efforts to model human mental processes are not concerned with the details of brain architecture. In fact a surprising number of programmers – sharing Margaret Boden's 'tin-can' image of computers – are not much interested in hardware of any sort. For example, efforts to simulate cognition (eg Eden et al, 1980) can proceed quite happily without any reference to the human cerebral equipment. It has become fashionable in some quarters to regard the mind as analogous to computer software, the brain as analogous to the physical computer circuits. This view – which should not be examined too closely – does suggest that human mental processes can be represented in software, without much thought having to be given to the physical machines on which the programs are to run.

We have already charted (Chapter 1) some of the links between the mental and computer worlds, links which are inevitably becoming more numerous with the development of expert systems. We are accustomed to seeing software promoted as able to 'process ideas', a clear analogue to what happens in the human brain. A package (eg MacPaint – Benzon, 1985) can be a 'tool for thinking'; and even a simple Scrabble or chess program can request 'thinking time'. With one software innovation after another, the links between the artificial system and the intelligent biological configuration become more apparent – and this represents something more than mere verbal slight of hand. There are immense difficulties in, for example, programming computers to relate images to real objects (Blake, 1984) or in enabling computers to acquire language skills (Naylor, 1984), but the progress is evident. Already computers are effective diagnostic physicians and competent analysts of geological data and new chemical compounds. They also compare well with human beings in many specific information processing and retrieval tasks (for example, Marcus, 1983, has experimentally compared the effectiveness of computers and humans as search intermediaries).

It is often pointed out that computer intelligence is a very limited commodity, that even if machines have really embarked upon the AI road there is still a long way to go. Computers need to have, for example, a modicum of common sense before they can be expected to tackle real-world problems. There *are* efforts to develop such humanlike qualities in machines, and it is significant that such attempts are proceeding in conjunction with an examination of the analagous features in human beings. As our understanding of mental processes grows, we are increasingly able to build equivalent functions into artefacts. This is directly relevant to the developing potential of expert systems.

EXPERT SYSTEMS

Definitions and Classifications

There are many definitions of expert systems: some simply list their features (knowledge base, inference engine, etc); others try to highlight particular programming features (eg use of logic programming techniques); and yet others focus on the supposed mental attributes of expert systems. It is possible to acknowledge the practical value of expert systems without being committed to a 'hard AI' line. The spectrum of definitions of expert systems therefore ranges from the suggestion that the new facilities are little more than a variation on traditional techniques of information storage and retrieval to the idea that at last the thinking machine is with us.

In one definition (quoted by d'Agapeyeff, 1983) expert systems are:

'problem solving programs that solve substantial problems

generally conceded as being difficult and requiring expertise. They are called knowledge-based because their performance depends critically on the use of facts and heuristics used by experts'.

The body of facts constitutes the effective knowledge of the system, and the heuristics are generally regarded as akin to the 'rules of thumb' used by human beings in circumstances where it would be impractical – possibly because of the 'combinatorial explosion – to reach a solution by means of a step-by-step logical procedure. The program uses the heuristics to operate on the stored knowledge in the light of a user enquiry, and ideally the system can explain its reasoning to the human operator.

The British Computer Society's Committee of the Specialist Group on Expert Systems has opted for the following definition of an expert system:

'the embodiment within a computer of a knowledge-based component from an expert skill in such a form that the machine can offer intelligent advice or take an intelligent decision about a processing function. A desirable additional characteristic, which many would regard as fundamental, is the capability of the system on demand to justify its own line of reasoning in a manner directly intelligible to the enquirer. The style adopted to attain these characteristics is rule-based programming'.

This definition emphasises an aspect of programming, allows for a wide range of applications, and indicates the desirability of an 'explanation-of-reasoning' capability. We see that expert systems can exploit various types of inference (not only first-order deductive logic) to operate on specialist knowledge of many different types.

In one simple definition, Johnson (1984), after suggesting that expert systems can most usefully be regarded as a software methodology, proposes that an expert system is:

'A computer system which emulates human expertise by making deductions from given information using the rules of logical inference'.

Following this definition we may assume that the inference procedures elicit information that is contained, albeit in a disguised form, in statements (rules) held in the knowledge base. In this way the expert system works to retrieve information, though in ways that are often different to those that characterise traditional information retrieval methods.

One view of expert systems is that they represent enhancements to an information retrieval system. Addis (1982), for example, adopts this approach in comparing an industrial database, a diagnostic aid and a medical consultation system. (As a subsidiary theme it is argued that expert systems should be used to communicate group practices to trained users rather than simulating experts to aid novices.)

Traditional information retrieval helps users to extract relevant information from a large pool of facts (eg documents characterised by index terms). In practice it has proved difficult to satisfy user requests by combining the index terms in Boolean or other types of algebraic expressions. One problem is that the words used to denote the required features are often ambiguous, and attempts to refine the request can often result in the systems producing no output whatsoever. One approach to this problem is 'to create a model of the documentation set in such a way that it is homomorphic with respect to user requests'. Such a model extends beyond index terms to cover relationships, to cope with data structures similar to semantic nets, sometimes used for knowledge representation in expert systems. In this way there is an evident evolutionary convergence of traditional information retrieval theory and the concepts underlying the (supposedly) newer disciplines of artificial intelligence in general and expert systems in particular.

Attempts to define expert systems and to show their kinship with particular traditional data processing methods (eg information retrieval) highlight differences between particular expert systems, ie some expert systems satisfy some definitions better than others. Addis (1982), for example, suggests that there are three major categories of expert systems. In the first class, the systems can only provide answers that have been clearly recorded beforehand (as, for example, in the CRIB system). The second class of expert systems allows simple fact interpolation where rules are used to generate new facts that can be used. Here the rules are insufficient to deduce, for example, new diseases or to recommend new medical treatments. In the third class is simple fact extrapolation where new rules of discovery can be generated. There are few, if any, candidates in this class, though the mathematical system AM is a candidate (Lenat, 1977). Each higher type of expert system contains all the mechanisms of the lower types.

In another categorisation of expert systems (highlighted by Alty and Coombs, 1984), Stefik et al (1982) classify expert systems according to how well they can cope with problems that are not 'well structured'. Here we can regard a well structured problem, ie one ideally suited to efficient automatic solution, as one in which the search space is small, the domain knowledge is reliable, and the data provided by the user is reliable and static over time.

Where such conditions obtain, there are a number of advantages. Programs can be handled by the machine in a straightforward fashion without the need for complex control strategies; a simple exhaustive search of the space will predictably generate a solution; and it is relatively easy to represent the domain knowledge. In such circumstances, accurate conclusions can be obtained, the procedures being able to rely on constant data throughout the generation of the solution. The Stefik (et al) approach has influenced how Alty and Coombs ordered relevant chapters dealing with examples of expert systems, viz:

— rule-based diagnostic systems for reasoning from uncertain data and knowledge (MYCIN and Prospector);

— associative and causal approaches to diagnosis (INTERNIST and CASNET);

— reducing large search spaces through factoring (Heuristic DENDRAL and Meta-DENDRAL);

— handling large search spaces through the use of abstraction (RI and MOLGEN).

There are clues in this approach to classifying expert systems as to the problems that are likely to be faced by microcomputers in this area. For example, what constitutes a small search space for a mainframe may be completely unmanageable for a micro. Software control strategies that may be quite unnecessary on a large machine may be essential if a system is to run on a microcomputer. This suggests that any classification of expert systems is likely to be mediated by the hardware context, with the corollary that if the 'lowest grade' of expert system is the only one suited to micros then we should not be too optimistic about the possibility of fully-fledged expert systems migrating to micros, despite the manifest trends charted in Chapter 2.

Software Impact

We have seen that expert systems can be regarded as a software methodology. A necessary element in the methodology is an enhanced provision for symbolic processing, aided by the development of the AI-related languages (see Choice of Languages, below). At the same time there has been growing pressure to develop appropriate software for micros, using either dialects of Prolog and Lisp or new approaches to exploiting the languages, such as Basic (see, for example, Naylor, 1983; James, 1984), that micros are accustomed to handling. A further, perhaps unexpected consequence of AI developments has been an acceleration of software development (Wess, 1984).

It has been found that AI concepts can be useful to the designers of commercial data processing systems. The time required to customise and later modify a software package can be significantly reduced. For example, Information Architects Inc (Needham Heights, Mass) has exploited expert systems technology to produce a customised, transaction-processing package. The basic standard commercial package was written in COBOL but portions of the new custom software were written in Prolog. The result was a satisfactory product using a combination of languages and development approaches.

The developers surveyed general business modules written in COBOL for real-time transaction processing, having good documentation, and also including development tools such as audit trails, files and a screen generator. Finally the Xerox PRAXA package, with 100,000 lines of code and occupying 10M bytes of mass memory, was selected from 15 possible choices. Three programming languages – COBOL, Datatrieve (DEC's database query language and report generator), and Prolog – were used to develop the custom software.

The impact of expert-systems developments on attitudes to software thus has various aspects. Languages are being evolved to satisfy the semantic and syntactical requirements of symbol processing, knowledge representation, etc; and to satisfy the processing scope of machines of different sizes. Also there is the impact on commercial software products: in addition to the generation of mainstream AI packages, the development of traditional packages is being increasingly influenced by expert-systems tools.

Architecture

There are various ways of representing the typical architecture of an expert system (Figure 4.1). In its most familiar form, an expert system is characterised by three basic elements: the Knowledge Manager, the Knowledge Base and the Situation Model (these are shown in Figure 4.1a which includes alternative names found in the literature). The Knowledge Base holds information that can be used by the Knowledge Manager to interpret the current contextual data in the Situation Model. Specialist knowledge pertaining to a particular subject area is carried in the Knowledge Base, whereas the Knowledge Manager is independent of specific subjects and can be used as a multi-application tool (see also Shells, below). A much quoted example to illustrate the distinction is that of MYCIN. This system's original Knowledge Base was constructed to allow the system to diagnose and treat bacterial infections, but it was found possible to develop EMYCIN (or Empty-MYCIN) as a Knowledge Manager to cope with problems in other subject areas, a different Knowledge Base being constructed in each case as appropriate.

Where the Knowledge Base in a particular field is comprehensive there is less demand upon the inferential logic of the Knowledge Manager when the system is interrogated and an answer is required: a search may quickly yield the necessary information, and inference procedures may not be required. Here a system may be regarded as powerful, even though there is only a relatively

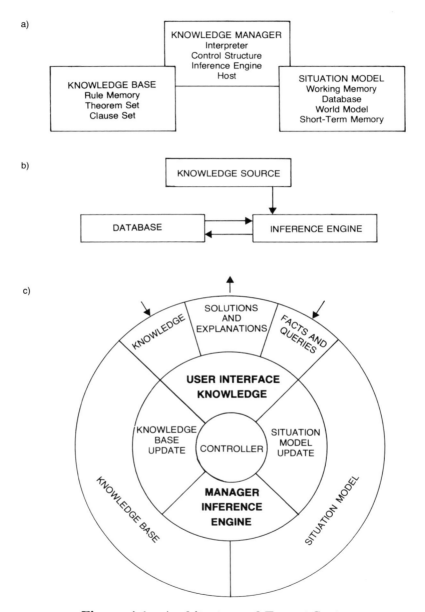

Figure 4.1 Architecture of Expert System

primitive inference capability. But it is obvious that a powerful system of this sort is scarcely an expert system: traditional information retrieval (IR) methods can produce satisfactory answers in circumstances where inference activity is not required. (The user, of course, may not be interested in whether he is dealing with an expert system or a standard IR facility: he simply wants a reply to his enquiry.)

There are few signs in Figure 4.1a that the expert system interacts with the outside world. In fact the Knowledge Manager is also concerned with knowledge acquisition, with the appropriate handling of information fed in by the user or acquired automatically (as, for example, via sensors in robot systems). In Figure 4.1b we see that a knowledge source is required but there is no suggestion here that the system is required to produce results as output. The generation of solutions and explanations is shown in Figure 4.1c, along with the dispositions of the main elements in the architecture. It is useful to bear in mind that expert systems are not self-contained worlds, indifferent to the circumstances of their subject domain. Ideally, with an operating expert system, able to provide solutions and to evolve to meet new demands, there is a constant two-way flow of information via an interface (see below).

Shells

There is increasing reference in the literature and in suppliers' brochures, to 'expert system shells'. These are generally regarded as knowledge engineering tools that include most of the elements necessary for building a complete expert system. Put briefly, and with some distortion:

a shell + specialist knowledge = an expert system

The intention is that shell systems should attract applications from many different subject areas. Basic inference procedures, for example, are universal, whether used in medical diagnosis, chemical analysis or military planning. The emergence of shells is one of the key developments allowing the creation of expert systems for microcomputers (see Chapter 5), and so injecting AI-related products into the mass market.

A shell system usually comprises tools to build the knowledge base (in any required subject area), an inference engine for logically processing the knowledge input, and an enquiry system to access the compiled knowledge and to apply it to real-world problems. We have seen that the Knowledge Manager (an effective shell) can be based on the rules developed for a dedicated expert system (eg MYCIN). Other shells are based on rules evolved for other dedicated systems (eg Prospector), or may be evolved from scratch with no expert-system precedent.

Most of the early shells derived from specific expert system applications and tended to have a relatively primitive inference mechanism. For example, shells derived from diagnostic systems (eg EMYCIN from MYCIN) tend to rely solely on *backward chaining* methods where the system works back from a conclusion or goal to see if the conditions which would make it true are satisfied – an appropriate ploy where, as in diagnostic systems, the possible conclusions can be specified in advance. A few of the earlier systems (eg Rutger University's Expert) offered *forward chaining* – where conclusions are deduced from available facts. Today, the emerging systems (eg Kee from IntelliGenetics, Loops from Xerox, Art from Inference Corporation) offer a variety of inference mechanisms. A central aim is to provide an effective development environment for expert systems.

The most powerful expert-system shells are usually intended to run on special-purpose workstations. Again Kee, Loops and Art are examples, and also S.1 from Teknowledge – all intended to operate on Lisp environments. (Lisp was developed to simplify the creation of expert systems and other symbol-processing languages, and for this purpose is specifically directed at the basic set of list-processing operations: match, join, link, substitute, etc. In this context, Lisp machines have been developed as personal computers able to perform the basic set of list-processing functions assumed by Lisp programs. For this reason, Lisp machines are well equipped to run expert systems and they are relatively cheap compared with general-purpose mainframe computers.)

Another group of shells are intended for specific mainframe computers, and may be written in traditional algorithmic languages such as Pascal or Fortran. Here the shells, directed at standard equipment, are run in a compiled form. After a change in the knowledge base, a compilation run is required to translate the knowledge-base/inference-engine structure into new and appropriate algorithms. This implies that shells in this category are not well suited to a highly interactive environment.

A growing sector of suppliers are now offering shells intended to run on microcomputers. Again it is worth emphasising that such shells, often directed at the IBM Personal Computer, have obvious limitations when compared with systems intended for mainframes. Systems shells intended for micros include MicroExpert, APES, ES/P Advisor, Expert-Ease and M.1 (see Chapter 5). The provision of shells for small computers is particularly important in the context of popular computing. There are immense social implications in making AI-related advisory and consultancy systems available on a mass-market basis.

Knowledge Engineering

Expert systems are 'expert' by virtue of containing specialist knowledge in some field. Thus they, like their human counterparts, are *expert in* geology or mathematics or car maintenance. It is no accident that most depictions of the typical architecture of an expert system show a Knowledge Base and Knowledge Manager, where the Knowledge Manager is expected to control and otherwise manipulate the specialist knowledge contained in the Knowledge Base. Knowledge engineering may thus be regarded as having two main elements:

— *knowledge elicitation,* where the specialist information is gleaned from a human expert prior to being fed into the Knowledge Base;

— *knowledge representation,* where the knowledge is stored in ways that are most appropriate for problem solution in a particular field.

Knowledge is elicited by a knowledge engineer, whereupon it is supplied in an appropriate form to a programmer (or team of programmers). This newly emerging procedure is fraught with difficulties. Experts may not be co-operative, they may have difficulty in articulating their expertise, there may be problems in identifying crucial heuristics, and it may not be clear how the findings can be best presented for the generation of program code. Advice can be given to the knowledge engineer as he embarks upon his task (see, for example, Feigenbaum and McCorduck, 1984), but such advice is inevitably subject to the very constraints that make it difficult for the expert in any field to express his expertise in a way that facilitates subsequent efficient coding. The knowledge engineer himself will evolve his own heuristics. Perhaps when the field is more mature, these will be easily identified (see also Simons, 1984, Chapter 5).

Once the expert's knowledge has been elicited, in one way or another, by the knowledge engineer, it is necessary to decide upon some appropriate formalism for the representation of the findings. Again the problem is compounded in various ways. There are, for example, many different types of knowledge (eg knowledge of objects, actions, events, performance, and of knowledge itself, ie knowing the limitations of what we know), and thus a representation formalism appropriate for knowledge of facts, say, is unlikely to be suitable for knowledge about performance (ie knowledge 'how to').

There are many different ways of representing knowledge. It is worth highlighting the most common ones:

— *First-order logic*
This is a formal method of representing logical propositions and the relations between them. For example, the familiar syllogistic propositions 'all men are mortal' and 'Socrates is a man' can be represented, where x is a variable, by *All* x *Mortal* (x) *If Man* (x) and *Man (Socrates)*. Moreover the system could infer from these expressions that Socrates is mortal. It is convenient for many purposes to represent logical propositions in this way, but for other tasks other representation formalisms are necessary;

— *Semantic networks*
Here it is possible to represent abstract relations among objects in the system's knowledge domain (eg membership of a class or set). Semantic networks have *nodes* (to represent objects, concepts, situations, etc) and *arcs* (that link the nodes). In a graphical representation, the arcs can be given arrows to indicate the direction in which a valid deduction

can be made. The relative simplicity with which correct deductions can be made, once a semantic network has been generated, is one of the reasons for the popularity of this representation method;

— *Frames*
These may be regarded as prototypes that represent objects by certain standard properties and relations to other objects. A frame is essentially a semantic network in which objects are represented by frames instead of by atomic symbols. This approach derives from a seminal 1974 paper by Marvin Minsky who suggested that a knowledge base can be broken into modular chunks ('frames'). Each frame is a data structure for representing a stereotypical situation. As with a typical semantic network, a frame comprises a network of nodes and relations, but organised in such a way that the top levels of the network represent elements that are always true whereas the lower levels have terminal nodes that must be filled with specific data. Frames have been developed to assist applications in such areas as computer vision and natural language understanding;

— *Production rules*
These were originally proposed as models of human reasoning, configured with an antecedent (to represent some pattern) and a consequent (to specify an action to be taken when the data matches the pattern). Typically the antecedent contains several clauses linked by the logical operators AND and OR, with the consequent containing verb phrases that specify the required action. For example *if* a is true *and* b is true *then* do c. In some cases the consequent can be a conclusion, a further inferred proposition to which a probability may be attached and which can be added to the knowledge base. Rule manipulation, a highly flexible realm, can involve common sense features, strategies for heuristic reasoning, etc.

The various representation formalisms have characteristic advantages. Production rules are well suited for representing procedural knowledge (ie methods for accomplishing goals) whereas semantic networks are good at representing factual relations between items. Modern approaches to knowledge representation tend to favour the simultaneous use of several formalisms in the same system.

Uncertainty

The requirement that computers behave in a more humanlike way has encouraged researchers to examine the question of uncertainty. In human activities ranging from the use of common sense to the deployment of expertise, uncertainty is often a crucial factor. There are frequent instances where a decision has to be made, or a problem solved, in circumstances where the available information is incomplete or hazy. This makes it difficult to frame nice algorithms in all the cases where effective results need to be obtained.

The uncertainty factor is closely related to the question of knowledge representation. Thus Zadeh (1983), a pioneer in this area, suggests that the representation of commonsense knowledge – one case where uncertainty needs to be considered – can be based on the assumption that the relevant propositions are *dispositions*, ie propositions with implied fuzzy quantifiers. *Fuzzy logic* has been developed to aid approximate or fuzzy reasoning (following Zadeh's 1965 paper). In this approach, fuzzy logic is seen as having two principal components:

— a translation system for representing the meaning of propositions and other semantic entities;

— an inferential system for answering a question that relates to the information in the knowledge base.

In a typical implementation, that developed in MYCIN and followed by other expert systems, a 'model of inexact reasoning' uses equations that function in the same way as expressions belonging to fuzzy sets. This involves membership values being regarded as certainty factors which are assigned constraints. In contrast to normal database conventions, a feature can be multivalued (ie regarded as fuzzy for particular purposes).

There are many conventions in ordinary language that allow subtle (and fuzzy) distinctions to be made between the characteristics of objects and people. Thus we can say that the colour of a car is 'blue*ish*' or that a person is *'more or less'* hostile to a particular idea. To embody fuzziness, a colour may be represented in a computer program as (Colour (Red 0.7)(Orange 0.3)) or as (Colour 6000), where 6000 denotes the wavelength of the light. In one representation, Shaket (1976) describes a technique able to convert physical values to (un)certainty values. Then it is possible to modify these – using linguistic devices such as 'very', 'sort of', etc – to shift the appropriate fuzzy set values in line with what might be expected by a human being.

The fuzzy-logic approach to expert systems has allowed the incorporation of an element of common sense and the provision of a decision-making ability in the absence of complete knowledge. Not all expert systems can handle uncertainty in their own subject domain, but increasingly a capacity for some degree of fuzzy reasoning is being regarded as part of the definition of the most competent expert systems. This applies to systems intended for microcomputers as well as to those intended to run on mainframes. And the provision of an element of 'uncertainty competence' has relevance for computer performance in many different application areas.

Jain and Haynes (1982), for example, show how fuzzy set theory can be used to solve problems in computer vision systems, and a dynamic scene system is introduced to illustrate the approach. (This work is important to the development of new-generation robots equipped with sensory capabilities.) Here it is proposed that computer vision systems 'should exploit approximate reasoning, opportunistic procrastination, and knowledge (both domain-dependent and domain-independent)'. And what is true of vision in robots is equally true for all tasks to be performed by computer-based systems in conditions of uncertain knowledge.

Inference

We have seen that an *inference engine* is invariably regarded as one of the central components in an expert system: it is this component that provides the system with its effective thinking power. In a conventional computer program there is no provision for an infer-ence capability. Ideally every possibility has been anticipated and, bugs apart, the system will behave predictably whatever the operating circumstances. However, with the knowledge-based system all the possible responses are *not* anticipated: various program actions and most conclusions have to be derived ('deduced', 'inferred') afresh from the facts and production rules contained in the knowledge base.

Various mechanisms can be included in the inference engine to allow the appropriate conclusions to be derived. Typically, three principal inference mechanisms are normally identified: backward chaining, forward chaining (both already mentioned) and inheritance. Backward chaining, for example, is a key feature in Prolog, and served as the most common inference mechanism in the early expert systems. It is obvious that backward chaining can only work reliably where all the possible goals or hypotheses can be determined in advance. Similarly, forward chaining quickly becomes unmanageable unless an effective strategy is provided to guide the computer from the stored premises to a useful conclusion. The *inheritance* play, characteristic of Prospector, uses a knowledge representation network in which spaces inherit the attributes of other spaces of which they are instances (eg the relation that biotite is a form of mica, which is a silicate, which is a mineral, and so biotite shares in the general properties of micas, silicates and minerals). This is reckoned to be a much more effective way of storing and changing knowledge than by providing an explicit statement for every case.

In addition to the three most obvious inference mechanisms, a variety of other reasoning ploys are being developed for expert systems. These, in part, are influenced by cognitive findings about how human beings solve problems of different types. The most sophisticated expert systems, not those found on micros, are likely to contain a variety of reasoning mechanisms that can be called up according to the character of the particular task being performed.

Interfaces

An effective human/machine interface is essential to an operating expert system, whatever its size or type: it is no use an expert system drawing startling conclusions from the information in its knowledge base if it does not let us know what they are, and similarly it is no use a system having prodigious reasoning abilities if we cannot ask it to employ them for our benefit. We need to be able to ask an expert system to provide us with answers; and interrogation and response are a two-way process.

The system should also be able to prompt the user for information about the problem, and in some cases the system may also request a numeric certainty factor indicating the user's confidence in the information supplied. It is also desirable for the user to be able to interrupt the process at any time to ask how a particular machine-generated conclusion has been reached.

The use of production rules makes it relatively easy for the system to generate prompts. The rule's condition can simply be turned into a question. For instance, the rule

> IF the patient has a temperature greater than 100 degrees
> THEN the patient has a fever

can prompt the question 'Is the patient's temperature greater than 100' by a straightforward operation on the words in the condition. Similarly, the use of rules can also make it easy to generate explanations. When, for example, a user is asked for more information, the system is simply trying to establish the conclusion of a rule. Hence a slight modification to the rule gives the user the required explanation.

It is conventional to regard the human/computer interface as comprising a keyboard and screen, though many other devices and facilities are now available – mice, touch-sensitive screens, voice response, etc. Now we recognise that artificial intelligence will increasingly shape the interfaces of the future. Speech input/ output will remove the need for keyboards and screens, and computers will become humanlike conversationists. It is inevitable that expert systems will be in the vanguard of such developments.

DEVELOPING EXPERT SYSTEMS

The approach to developing conventional software is well established, though refinements and modifications to the underlying methods are constantly discussed. It may be thought, in these circumstances, that expert systems – after all, a species of software – could be developed in the traditional way. However, a consensus is emerging to the effect that expert systems are not well suited to the familiar software development cycle. For example, Sagalowicz (1984) refers to 'important differences' between the typical software development cycle and the process of developing a knowledge-based system.

It is possible to identify methods that are useful in identifying problems that are suitable for a knowledge-based solution, and ways of assessing the associated technical risks and potential payoffs. When such factors have been considered, it is feasible to embark upon a system development cycle that can be regarded as comprising the phases of demonstration prototyping, system development and operational integration. The prototyping phase enables the knowledge engineer to grasp the scale of the project and to estimate the resources required. Feasibility can also be demonstrated at this time, allowing a budget and a plan for system development to be defined. Now the prototype can be expanded to meet the requirements of the full application. Finally the system is established in its actual working environment, documentation is developed, end-users are trained, and a maintenance group is created.

In another approach to systems development (Durham, 1984), the first of three overlapping phases corresponds to conventional systems analysis; the second involves system design; and finally the system is implemented. This follows the development by Annie Brooking (of South Bank Polytechnic, England) of a methodology for designing knowledge-based systems that compares with the Yourdon method of structured systems analysis. There is no reason to think that a systematic method for developing knowledge-based facilities cannot be developed, though it would be unwise to rely solely upon the traditional approach to software production.

CHOICE OF LANGUAGES

General

Traditional programming languages have not proved to be well suited to computer applications in artificial intelligence in general and expert systems in particular. We sometimes encounter talk of expert systems written in Cobol or Pascal or (with an eye on the massive personal-computer sector) Basic, but such languages are far from ideal in representing the real-world knowledge required by many AI systems or in providing the flexible exploratory style needed by programmers in a highly unpredictable new area. It is largely the emergence of new programming tools that has stimulated the development of AI-related systems.

Lisp and Prolog

Special languages, notably Lisp and Prolog, have been developed to facilitate the programming of AI applications. Such tools are often dubbed 'descriptive' or 'logic programming' languages, though Lisp is historically rooted in mainstream computational theory whereas Prolog derives in part from formal logic. (Lisp, signalling LISt Programming language, has also been described as Lots of Infuriatingly Stupid Parentheses, on account of how brackets proliferate in the source code.) Lisp can be traced back to a 1956 conference, the first on AI, at Dartmouth College. John McCarthy (of MIT), who attended the conference, first developed FLPL, added an If-Else construct, and in due course Lisp emerged.

The Lisp language is very popular in the US, though Prolog is favoured in the UK, Europe and Japan. One trend is for practical programming environments to supplement the underlying implementation languages by overlaying more English-like languages for knowledge representation and by integrating extra facilities into the system. Though some traditional languages (eg Pascal, C, Fortran, Basic, etc) have been used to implement expert systems, the advantages of using logic programming facilities are becoming more generally recognised. Conventional languages have been used for some of the small expert systems, but most of the larger ones have been written in Lisp or in Lisp-based languages such as OPS5. At the same time there are disadvantages in using Lisp: it is, for example, best suited to an expensive workstation or superminicomputer, and it is not the easiest tool to use (Lisp experts are still in relatively short supply). Prolog is usually regarded as much easier for a novice to understand, though this language too has various disadvantages.

It can be difficult in Prolog to provide the necessary procedural information for completing a task in an efficient manner, rendering large Prolog programs difficult to comprehend and maintain.

Moreover, unlike the case with Lisp, there is no really adequate programming environment yet available for Prolog – though the adoption by the Japanese of Prolog as their 'kernel' language may well soon alter this. One solution is for integrated systems, partaking of the characteristics of both Lisp and Prolog, to overcome the respective disadvantages of each. Again we can cite Loops, the Xerox environment which integrates four different programming approaches under Interlisp-D.

Lisp has been represented as an effective language singularly well suited to AI implementations. Prolog, however, is also an expert system shell including a knowledge representation structure and an inference engine. Specific advantages claimed for Prolog over Lisp, bearing in mind that, strictly speaking, like is not being compared with like, include the following (cited by Johnson, 1984):

— Prolog allows a program to be formulated in smaller units, the multiple nesting of function definitions in Lisp preventing easy comprehension;

— Prolog provides the programmer with generalised record structures and an elegant mechanism for manipulating them;

— Prolog programs can be written without the need for implementation-oriented concepts. These are frequently necessary in Lisp, but involve language extensions, again impairing readability.

There is a continuing debate between the respective advocates of Lisp and Prolog (see, for example, Johnson, 1984, pp 97-121; and Foster, 1984). The respective advantages and disadvantages of the two languages are widely agreed (eg the simplicity of Prolog and its inefficiency in searching a large knowledge base), and there is a consensus that neither language, taken in isolation, suits everyone. Efforts to integrate the two languages, or to develop dialects superior to either, have proceeded on several parallel tracks.

For example, LM-Prolog, developed at the University of Uppsala in Sweden, allows Prolog researchers to use development tools for Lisp environments (Professor Tarnlund observes that when 'people develop expert systems in Lisp or other programming languages they are really implicitly developing a Prolog system'). Similarly Alan Robinson, at Syracuse University, NY, is developing a version of an integrated language called Super-LOGLISP. And the dialect approach is also gaining favour when it may be inappropriate to use pure Prolog. Poplog, another option, has been developed as a programming environment that can support three different languages: POP-II, Lisp and Prolog (see Ramsay, 1984; Sloman et al, 1983).

The Poplog facility, developed at the University of Sussex, combines the POP-II and Prolog languages in the same address space and so provides the procedural effectiveness of POP and the clarity of knowledge representation evident in Prolog. The final version of Poplog was an extended version to include Lisp, though the Lisp implementation is largely restricted to teaching. Poplog is supplied directly to academic users by the University of Sussex, with commercial marketing carried out by System Designers Ltd. By 1984 there were around two dozen industrial and commercial installations and about four dozen educational ones with customers throughout Europe.

The language trends are evident. Lisp and Prolog will continue to be used for a wide variety of AI implementations, including expert systems. Integrated environments (LM-Prolog, Super-LOGLISP, Interlisp-D, etc) will try to capture the respective advantages of the two main AI languages; and dialects will evolve to exploit particular applications and machine sectors (for example, some dialects will focus on micro usage). Efforts will continue to be made in mainstream languages, if only because of the reservoir of established programmer expertise, to produce expert systems and other AI-related products. Relatively primitive expert systems will continue to be written in Basic to exploit the massive personal-computer sector.

EXPERT SYSTEMS AND MICROS

Various approaches have been adopted to enable micros to encroach on the performance domains of minicomputers and mainframes (see Chapter 2). One ploy is architectural: for example, micros can acquire effective mini and mainframe power by being configured in a large parallel array (as, for instance, with the transputer). Or a software approach can be adopted, of particular relevance to the design of AI-related products. It is now practical to implement Prolog and Lisp versions on microcomputers. For example, Expert Systems Ltd is now implementing Prolog-1 on the IBM Personal Computer and other machines based on the Intel 8088/8086 microprocessor.

To develop the 8086 Prolog, the company bought a program to translate from Z80 assembler to 8086 assembler, though the program was found to be unsatisfactory for various reasons. The company then wrote its own translator in Prolog. Various features have been added to the new Prolog version, including floating point capabilities, direct access file handling, and user error-control. Today versions of Prolog are available on a wide range of Z80- and 8088-based micros, as well as on PDP-11s and VAXs.

Two approaches to Prolog on micros have been identified: the Prolog-1 approach, considered the more commercially oriented, and Frank McCabe's micro-Prolog (see Pountain, 1984). Micro-Prolog is equipped with a number of friendly shells for the beginner, and it is possible to develop quite large projects on a small CP/M micro. The dialect was originally developed at Imperial College to run on the Z80, and was tested on 10-year-old children during a project called 'Logic as a Computer Language for Children'.

The first micro-Prolog appeared in 1982, written for CP/M 2.2 systems. Since that time, versions have appeared for the Sinclair Spectrum, the Acorn BBC Micro, and various 8088-based systems (including the IBM Personal Computer operating under MS-DOS or CP/M-86). It seems likely that Prolog versions will become available, by one route or another, for most of the personal computers on the market.

In 1984 Microsoft Inc, a company that focuses on producing microcomputer languages and operating systems, announced an upgraded version of its muLisp version of Lisp. The new muLisp 82 is able to run on 16-bit microcomputers based on the 8088 and 8086 processors (used, for example, in IBM PCs and IBM-compatible PCs); muLisp is described as an 'Artificial Intelligence Development System' (it is described in detail in *Expert Systems,*

Vol. 1, No. 2, pp 108-109). King (1984) considers how Lisp can run on a 'standard supermicro', consisting of a microprocessor such as the Motorola 68000 with between 500K byte – 1M byte of RAM and a 40M byte disk drive. Such a machine would provide 'the equivalent of a minicomputer service' and offer 'many exciting possibilities'. Two examples are given: REDUCE (to manipulate algebraic equations) and Plant Doctor (an expert system to diagnose house plant diseases).

Developments in both Prolog and Lisp show that AI-related implementations are now well within the province of microcomputers and supermicros. There may be debate about the extent to which artificial intelligence can be realised in low-end machines, just as there is debate in the larger AI controversy. But the trend is clear: as micros gain in competence, and AI-related languages and dialects become more flexible and adaptable, so the scope of microcomputers will grow. If effective expert systems can today be implemented on minis and mainframes it will soon be clear that they can also be implemented on microcomputers. There are enough suppliers to tell us that this is already the case.

SUMMARY

This chapter has highlighted some of the main features of expert systems, with attention given to definitions and classifications, architectural aspects, software, shells, knowledge engineering, uncertainty aspects, inference and interfaces. The task of developing expert systems, at some variance with the traditional software development cycle, is mentioned, and there is brief discussion of the choice of languages for AI-related products. We mentioned the on-going debate between the respective advocates of Lisp and Prolog, and signalled some of the ploys – dialects, new languages and integrated systems – being adopted to exploit the advantages of specific language formalisms.

Finally there is reference to how the mainstream AI languages – Lisp and Prolog – are becoming increasingly available on micros and supermicros, aided by new architectural configurations (eg a proliferation of micros operating in parallel). It is suggested that AI software will become widespread among users of personal computers. The migration of AI software to micros is already beginning to yield a plethora of commercial products (some of these are cited in Chapter 5), and there can be little doubt that the trend will continue.

5 Some Products and Companies

INTRODUCTION

A rapid expansion is now taking place in the supply of expert systems and AI-related products at all levels. In Europe, for example, expert systems of many different types are being made available for micros, minis and mainframes. Britain and France are leading countries in this development in the tradition, respectively, of Alan Turing's work in the 1940s and the early development of Prolog at the University of Marseilles. The rapid growth of the European expert systems field is taking place for two main reasons: a new realism about the scope and limitations of AI-related products, and the successful isolation of specific tasks that lend themselves to treatment by expert systems. In one estimate (Tate, 1984), there are now around 200 separate expert systems projects under way in Europe.

A wide spectrum of organisations are now sponsoring work in this area: for example, large user companies (Dutch Shell, ICI, etc), established computer companies (Siemens, ICL, Norsk Data, etc), start-up firms (some offshoots from specific academic projects), and universities are now involved. Funding initiatives, as we have seen, include the wide-ranging Alvey and Esprit programmes. Around $40 million was spent in Europe in 1984 on developing expert systems. Johnson (1984) estimates that the figure will have reached $200 million by 1990. Many of the European suppliers of expert systems are aiming their products at the custom sector. One example is ICI's development tool Savoir (see Spectrum of Activity, below); another is ICI's Counsellor, designed to diagnose and treat agricultural diseases.

Other European activities in this area include work by Helix to develop an expert system to help in car purchase, research by Elf Aquitaine and Schlumberger in geological prospecting, and work by such companies as Framentec (Monte Carlo), Cap Sogeti, Thomson CSF, Bull, Seri Renault and Matra. In November 1984 a conference was staged in Paris by the French Association of Artificial Intelligence and Simulation Systems (AFIAS) to explore the AI possibilities in manufacturing, a prime target for expert systems. In Germany, the University of Kaiserlautern is researching AI-related diagnostic applications in medicine, automobile service and manufacturing. Similarly, companies in Sweden (Epitec and Infologics) are exploring various expert-system development tools. In-house applications are being developed by Philips, Norsk Data, ICL, Nixdorf and Siemens. Many of these projects have had to overcome the inevitable doubts about the status of artificial intelligence and about the real commercial and practical value of AI-related development programmes. In these circumstances the emergence of small effective systems that can be seen to work has been helpful: a successful micro-based expert system suggests that funding for larger projects may also be worthwhile.

The value of small systems in this context has been emphasised by various observers. For example, in connection with simple expert systems, Alex d'Agapayeff notes that 'the task is modest, clear-cut, narrow in scope, noncritical, and tailored to fit an attainable solution'. This helps to combat the widespread idea that expert systems are necessarily 'complex, risky and demanding'. In the same vein, Johnson (1984) observes: 'Small systems are likely to attract sharply increased attention in the next year or two with some early commercial successes. Some small systems are already in practical application providing a positive feedback and encouraging the development and refinement of more systems of the same type'.

We have seen that one of the key factors influencing the availability of venture capital for AI-related projects is what has been called the 'Gosh, wow' overselling of possibilities in this area. The media, for example, always eager to arouse interest, have often stimulated unrealistic expectations. Eugene Pettinelli (quoted by Rose,1985), a general partner in Fairfield Venture Partners and a supporter of the successful AI company Symbolics Inc, has declared: 'I'm being very cautious right now because there is very little relationship between the hype and the real potential of AI technology, especially in expert systems'. One problem is the paucity of genuine expertise in the AI area: if there are so few computer people with AI competence, the interested venture capitalist is unlikely to have much insight into the development possibilities. Again it is worth emphasising that a demonstrably successful small expert system, running on, say, an IBM Personal Computer, can help to create the atmosphere in which investment funding for more ambitious projects will be made available.

In the US, various large corporations – General Motors, Boeing, Lockheed, Digital Equipment, Texas Instruments, etc – have recently made investments in AI companies. Harvey Newquist, consultant at DM Data Inc and editor of *AI Trends* newsletter, pointed out in early-1985 that 'most of the AI financing will come from the bigger companies'. There is a growing recognition that AI-related products will become increasingly important to large companies, both in their internal operations and the introduction of new products to the marketplace.

Artificial intelligence development will be stimulated, in part, by general progress in computer technology. Here a key factor will be the high speed of modern processors, a high rate of computation allied to relatively economic systems. For instance, David Ben-Daniel, executive vice president of Genesis Group International Inc, reckons that an important AI threshold will be reached when 50 million to 100 million instructions per second of computing power are available in the $50,000 to $100,000 range. This point has been taken in various research projects where, for example, efforts are being made to use Lisp to solve problems 'with lightning speed'. Durham (1984) describes work at the Massachusetts Institute of Technology (MIT) where a major problem will be to get 256,000 processors talking to each other.

The current commercial scene is a complex spectrum of competing interests and activities. Despite the reaction against hype and overselling, there is still an underlying conviction that the emerging AI scene is one of immense commercial potential. It is possible to identify some leading AI companies and products in the present market scene, though shifts are inevitable in such a relatively uncertain technological arena. For instance, Expert Systems International and Logic Programming Associates have been identified as the main UK contenders for the Prolog market, and many other products are on offer from other suppliers. Tymshare UK is offering Reveal, another language that can be used in developing expert systems, and various shells are available in the UK, some of the main ones being:

— AL/X from Intelligent Terminals;

— APES from Logic Based Systems;

— ES/P Advisor from Expert Systems International;

— M.1 and S.1 from Framentec;

— MicroExpert and Savoir from Isis Systems;

— Sage from Systems Designers.

It is significant that a number of these shells can be effectively implemented on microcomputers (see also Some Micro-Based Systems, below). AL/X, for example, will run on DEC PDP-11 systems, or on VAX computers or micros that will support a standard Pascal compiler. Sage has been implemented on DEC, ICL Prime and IBM PC systems. Similarly, APES and ES/P Advisor can also run on IBM Personal Computers. M.1 is an IBM PC-based shell, developed in the US by Teknowledge and marketed by Framentec. Intelligent Terminals and Export Software International (renamed Expert Software International just before it went into liquidation) launched various inductive shells – ACLS Expert-Ease, Extran-7 and Rulemaster – which can be implemented on CP/M microcomputers, the IBM PC, DEC PDP and VAX computers. Other systems – for example, TK!Solver (see Konopasek and Jayaraman, 1984) – while not, strictly speaking, expert systems, exhibit many kindred properties, and there is inevitable overlap between the categories.

Many of the expert systems mentioned so far (particularly in Chapter 3) have been produced to run on minicomputers, superminis and mainframes. In the present chapter, the emphasis has changed: it is worth highlighting the expert systems, shells, etc intended for microcomputers. This is a massive growth area, of immense significance for at least three reasons:

— micro-based expert systems, where clearly successful, can help promote more ambitious expert-system projects;

— micro-based expert systems have great commercial potential in their own right, targeted, as they are, on the vastly expanding personal-computer sector;

— micro-based expert systems, when available in many different implementations for the non-expert domestic user, will have profound social implications.

Some available micro-based expert systems are profiled in more detail below. First it is useful to indicate the range of AI-related activities in various companies. These activities will help to influence the shape of micro-based artificial intelligence, and AI generally, in the years to come.

COMPANY ACTIVITIES AND PRODUCTS

Much of the most useful current activity is in developing realistic (ie simpler) expert systems. In highlighting some aspects of the misleading media hype Alex d'Agapeyeff, in *A Short Survey of Expert Systems in UK Business*, remarks that 'there is a sad irony in the extent to which AI (while advocating and, indeed, achieving user-understandable computer programs) is itself associated with opaque jargon, off-putting anthropomorphic claims'. Another report (*Expert Systems: A Management Guide* by Mike Turner, Pactel director), published in December 1984, emphasises that the viability of expert systems has been proven in only a small number of cases. Furthermore, 'the limited experience of transforming a prototype into a cost-effective tool suggests that this is a non-trivial undertaking'; and again it is emphasised that a company selecting its first application should opt for a relatively cheap expert system shell or knowledge acquisition product. Such an approach has the obvious advantage that, with an effective inference engine supplied, the user need only focus on the development of an appropriate knowledge base.

The use of a modest, realistic expert-system shell suggests that software could be developed to run on a microcomputer, say an

IBM PC. In this context, a 'simpler expert system' has various identifiable features (following d'Agapeyeff):

— the system, possibly initiated as an exploration, has not needed to be cost-justified in advance;

— it is narrow in scope, and tailored to fit an attainable solution;

— it can be developed by a committed application specialist;

— it involves reasoning that can be undertaken with the selected inference engine;

— the input data, apart from dialogue with the user, has been previously validated.

The use of relatively simple expert systems with these types of features is increasingly common for a growing spectrum of applications, but not all new expert systems are simple in this sense. Beechhold (1985) describes Expert Choice, a 'tough to learn' but valuable piece of software aimed at helping executives to make decisions. This is effectively an expert system builder available for personal computers and deriving from the work of Thomas Saaty at the University of Pittsburgh. Here printed tutorials are run in conjunction with demonstration decision-making problems on disk – with the aim of reshaping the user's thinking.

The Reveal package (from Tymshare), already mentioned, provides a fully portable software environment for the development of knowledge-based systems. A rule-based programming language for representing knowledge as production rules is included, and there is provision for fuzzy sets and approximate reasoning techniques, necessary to cope with the uncertainty and ambiguity that characterises much of human thinking.

The English-language rule representation makes the rule base accessible to the domain experts providing the knowledge to build the system. This approach helps to ease the knowledge acquisition bottleneck and allows the knowledge base to be conceptually separate from the inference engine. It also allows multiple knowledge bases, perhaps derived from different sources, to be switched and compared. Various inference strategies can be employed (backward chaining, forward chaining, special purposes, etc). The flexibility of the Reveal system allows a wide range of business, scientific and educational users to explore knowledge engineering and to develop systems from the simplest of business models to highly sophisticated expert systems. In summary (and according to the sales blurb), Reveal

— is a powerful, easy-to-use integrated system;

— combines the capabilities of decision support systems with those of expert systems;

— uses natural English-like syntax;

— has an unrestricted range of control strategies;

— has a mainframe-to-micro link;

— is available on a wide range of computers.

As with other micro-based facilities (see Some Micro-Based Systems, below), Reveal can run on microcomputers. For example, the full system is available for the IBM PC XT with 640K. It also runs on IBM VM/CMS, VAX/VMS, ICL/VME and on Tymshare's own computers on a timesharing basis*.

Reveal is only one in a growing family of systems designed to help users build expert systems. ART, for example, from Inference Corporation, is rich in semantics to aid the task of knowledge encoding. A mechanism is included for the exploration of hypothetical alternatives and for modelling situations that change with time, and a flexible rule base facilitates the representation of human knowledge. An interactive development environment allows an interface to be developed with other programs already working in the Symbolics 3600 computing environment. An expert system can be introduced gradually, making use of software already there. Other systems worth mentioning are the Duck system, used for writing predicate-calculus rules; Arby software for writing expert systems for applications in diagnosis; and DC-3, for diagnosing electronic faults. Yet others are the MRS knowledge representation systems to help us to build expert systems, OPS5 to assist system building, and the OPS5-based RPMS to aid the control of NASA shuttle flight operations. SRL+, from the

* through TYMNET, Tymshare's International Telecommunications Network.

Carnegie Group, helps users to construct a broad range of knowledge-based systems, and TEAM is a natural language package (from Symbolics Inc) designed to be transportable from domain to domain by a 'domain expert' rather than by a linguistics or AI expert.

The Palo Alto (California) Teknowledge company has launched two system shells (both already mentioned): the large system S.1, planned initially for the Xerox 1100 and 1108 workstations; and the small system M.1, written for IBM PCs (and compatible microcomputers). M.1, costing around $12,500, is promoted as a complete knowledge engineering tool, especially designed for programmers who do not have previous experience of work in knowledge engineering or artificial intelligence. A central aim of M.1 is to allow users to explore expert-system possibilities at low cost.

As with Reveal and other systems, M.1 systems can be constructed using an English-like language for stating facts and rules about a specific application. An effective knowledge base can be created using any standard text editor or word processor whereupon it is loaded into M.1 for testing and debugging. A consultation front-end allows users to run the question-and-answer dialogue necessary for the solution of particular problems. Other M.1 features include an explanation facility, a multi-window display, interactive knowledge base debugging, and the provision of certainty factors in rules and questions. Teknowledge reckons M.1 to be a 'complete symbolic programming language'. Colour displays can be used and the system will accept abbreviated answers to its questions. M.1 runs on IBM PCs under the DOS 2 operating system, and requires 128K RAM. Again M.1 is one of many knowledge-based tools bringing expert-system development within the scope of the personal-computer user. Other examples are the numerous AI software packages produced by Digital Equipment Corporation for use on VAX and personal computers, and the MProlog systems (from Logicware, Toronto) written for the IBM PC.

Many of the micro-based shells are specifically designed for personal computers (most commonly, we see, for the IBM PC). Some shells, however, emerge as distillations of larger programs, originally designed for relatively large computers but then 'shoehorned' into the sorts of storage and processing capacity that are within the scope of low-end systems. This means that developments in knowledge engineering that are seemingly unrelated to small machines may quickly come to be relevant to the microcomputer sector. In this context it is worth highlighting two important recent developments:

— the Sperry Corporation, signing agreements with Texas Instruments and Intellicorp, has recently put together a $20 million effort to claim leadership of the AI and expert-systems sector. A massive Knowledge Systems Centre is to be opened in Minneapolis to handle commercial and defence markets. Sperry are to launch various AI-product programmes with Texas Instruments which in October 1984 launched a single-user Lisp-based personal computer, and Sperry will also distribute the Knowledge Engineering Systems from Intellicorp which produces a software in Menlo Park, California. The system will also be used to develop expert-systems products ('knowledgeware') for business and government applications;

— ICL and Systems Designers International claimed a new knowledge engineering advance in late-1984 with the production of a general-purpose expert systems shell. The program – to be sold by ICL as Advisor, and by Systems Designers as Envisage – allows the user to talk directly to the system. The shell was developed from Sages, a system developed by Systems Programmers for the 2900 series. Significantly, it is expected that the new system shell will percolate down to smaller machines in 1985.

These two developments show how business initiatives and product innovations can influence the implementation of AI-related applications on low-end machines: there can be a direct attack on the micro sector or large-system programs can be contracted for use in a wider user environment. The personal-computer scene will see products emerging in these and other ways.

There is a growing view that AI technology will find its main market among users of applications software. In this vein, Joseph Fox, chairman of Software Architecture and Engineering, suggests that AI's biggest sales will come from everyday computer use –

and we may infer that many of the applications will be geared to personal computers. Fox observes: 'If the AI applications market grows to $9 billion by 1995, as analysts predict, then demand for development tools [using expert-system technology] will reach $90 billion'. There are signs from other large companies that the applications-software sector, as a focus for AI products, is the correct one.

Thus Control Data Corporation aims to be the first computer maker to offer AI-based application development software as a standard system feature. In this connection CDC, having recently acquired 20% of SA & E stock, intends to launch with that company an upgrade of SA & E's main product, an applications generator used to build in-house expert systems. A key objective of the new venture is to move from selling to expert-systems houses to selling to the expert-systems users (Fox: 'We will then be in the mainstream of the scientific and data processing community, and we hope to be the leading supplier of inference engines and knowledge representation tools' – quoted by Berney, 1984).

The shifting focus of AI products will influence the development of various market sectors. Expert systems, designed specifically for micros or migrating from larger machines, will become increasingly available for the users of personal computers in the domestic, industrial and commercial environments. There will still be expert systems intended for top-end machines – in government, universities, industry and elsewhere – but low-end AI applications are sure to be a high growth area in the years to come. Already some micro-based expert systems and systems shells have had significant commercial success – and high exposure in the media. Before considering a selection of these, it is useful to glance at Lisp workstations, a sector that will influence the development of expert systems for micros and larger machines.

LISP WORKSTATIONS

There are various possible approaches to the development of expert systems (we have already seen that the traditional software development cycle is not applicable without at least a shift in emphasis). In one categorisation (Johnson, 1984), the various approaches to expert systems development include:

— using traditional languages on 'stock' hardware: for example, using Fortran running on IBM or DEC equipment, as at
Rutgers University;

— using a specific AI-related language – Lisp, Prolog or high-
level languages based on them – on stock hardware, as at
Carnegie Mellon University, and in most of the Prolog-
based developments in Europe;

— using Lisp on a special Lisp workstation, as in such companies as Apex and IntelliGenetics.

It is clear that the development options will proliferate in the
years ahead. The emerging family of Prolog workstations will
grow, and Lisp or Prolog units will link to conventional mainframes. We are also likely to witness the process whereby expert
systems themselves work out how best to design further expert
systems for particular purposes. The need for dedicated workstations has been highlighted by the fact that both Lisp and Prolog
tend to run inefficiently on machines with conventional architectures. There is now a wide range of Lisp workstations, produced by
such companies as Lisp Machines Inc (LMI), Symbolics and
Xerox, and costing between $3,500 (for the LMI Lambda Interlisp
package) and $129,500 (for the Xerox 1132-100 system), at
late-1984 prices.

The first Lisp workstations appeared in the early-1980s, and
Xerox was quick to see their relevance to the rapidly developing
office-automation market. 1981 saw the launch of the Xerox Dol-
phin system as the 1100 'scientific information processor', and at
the same time the LM-2 (Symbolics) and the Lisp Machine (Lisp
Machines Inc) were launched. Later Xerox launched the
Dandelion/1108 and the Dorado/1132 systems. These were some
of the early machines in the rapidly developing AI machine sector.
LMI introduced the Lambda system in 1983, and Symbolics began
shipments of the 3600 Lisp machine. F Stephen Wyle has pointed
out that by-products of AI research have included timesharing,
networking, windowing, and various software tools ('In a sense,
Lisp machines are another such product – a tool developed for AI
researchers that is usable for purposes not necessarily associated
with AI'). The Symbolics product line manager, Abe Hirsche, has
observed that the first forty customers for the 3600 Lisp machine

were interested in forty different applications – including computer-based training, artificial vision, and the design of video games.

Ideally, AI researchers should be able to work in a Lisp or Prolog environment with the necessary development tools available on an office desk. Corley and Statz (1985) describe the Explorer Lisp workstation that meets these requirements. In addition the system comes equipped with graphics tools, natural language interfaces, relational table managers, command interfaces, and knowledge engineering tools developed by the OEM and third-party vendors. The keyboard and display fit on a desk, and the CPU and disk drives can be sited nearby. Design features of the Explorer, from Texas Instruments, derive from the MIT CADR design that is also used in the AI workstations from Lisp Machine Inc.

The Lisp processor uses nine TI 74AS181 ALU integrated circuits and a lookahead carry generator. Sixteen high-speed binary arithmetic operations can be performed on two 32-bit words, and flexible micro-instruction formats enable the Lisp processor to operate on words, half-words, and bytes – a standard provision in the Explorer Common Lisp language environment. A number of other features – the window-oriented display editor, the advise facility, etc – are particularly useful to the AI researcher.

There is already a proliferation of Lisp workstations, with relatively few Prolog equivalents. The Lisp systems are available from the large established firms (LMI, Symbolics, Tektronix, Perq Systems, Xerox, TI, etc) and increasingly from new start-up enterprises. In these circumstances there is debate as to which software environment will prevail for designers needing symbolic processing workstations, though to a large extent the early firms have dictated the shape of this market sector. Texas Instruments is said to have sold hundreds of its new Lisp machines to MIT for delivery in 1985 and 1986 (see Hindin, 1985), and if potential users are convinced that Lisp systems are the way to go then in five years' time the sales could reach $2.5 billion ('no one knows what will happen if IBM or Digital Equipment Corporation opts for Lisp and symbolic processing workstations').

The preponderance of Lisp workstations makes it risky for

suppliers to run against the trend (the Japanese fifth-generation choice of Prolog as the 'kernel' language may influence this situation). The Tektronix symbolic processing environment is based on Xerox's Smalltalk-80 language, though Lisp and Prolog are available as options – all on the Motorola 68010 microprocessor. In fact it has been found that Lisp, used in isolation, is usually inefficient in workstation implementations, and it is conventional for the symbolic processing workstations to extend Lisp in various ways.

In the various software environments the IBM Personal Computer is ubiquitous ('It has become a personal productivity tool found almost everywhere'). And some companies (eg Xerox and Daisy Systems Corporation) have arranged for their workstations to link directly to IBM PCs. A personal computer to (Lisp) workstation link allows a machine (say, the Xerox 1108) to exploit the many PC peripherals and features (eg colour monitors and analogue/digital speech input). Similarly, the Daisy Personal Logician computer-aided engineering software runs on the IBM PC/XT and on the new Intel 32-bit 80286-based IBM PC AT.

We see increasing involvement of personal computers, at various levels, in the task of expert-system development. Links from dedicated Lisp machines to PCs are one way in which the production of knowledge-based systems can involve a wide sector of microcomputer users. In another context, expert systems and system shells are increasingly being made available for low-end machines. We have already mentioned several examples. It is worth highlighting other systems of this sort, some of which moreover have been much reported in both the general and technical literature.

SOME (MORE) MICRO-BASED SYSTEMS

General

Reviews of expert systems (or *putative* expert systems) appear frequently in the personal-computer journals. It is recognised that AI-related products are becoming increasingly relevant to the activities of hobbyists and other home computer users. Naylor (iii), 1984, for example, compares the claims of Hulk and Expert-Ease (this latter having been much discussed because of its association with Donald Michie and various commercial reverses). The aim in both cases is much the same, at least in the implementations that merit comparison – the program (Hulk or Expert-Ease) is provided with a sample of objects, whereupon a method of discrimination is automatically developed to allow the program to classify a range of objects in the group. For example, data could be supplied about the measurements of skeletons whose sex was known, whereupon the program would develop a system for sexing skeletons in general. And the approach is quite general: current limited data is supplied to allow the system to evaluate new instances or future possibilities.

The two systems are reckoned to be 'revolutionary in the micro marketplace' (see below for more details about Expert-Ease), allowing the user to carry out the discrimination tasks that are central to most expert systems. Expert-Ease (looking for rules and trying to offer perfect results) is more ambitious than Hulk (which simply makes it easier for the user to test rules that may already have been thought of), though Expert-Ease is much more expensive. A much cheaper Expert-Ease 'could become a best seller on a par with VisiCalc'.

These systems are characteristic of programs being offered for low-end machines – in particular for the IBM PC. Suppliers in the US, Europe and elsewhere are increasingly conscious of the commercial possibilities in the micro sector. For example, Information Engineering (Aust) Pty Ltd has recently (late-1984) announced the first in a series of products that will develop into an expert system generator for use on the IBM Personal Computer. The software development is supported by Business Loans & Equity Ltd, involving a $A600,000 grant from the Australian Industrial Research and Development Incentives Board (Airdib) and private investors. The software, marketed in the User range, will concentrate on the user's definition of his own data to enable the resulting expert system to exactly match the user's requirements (Mason, 1984).

Here it is emphasised that though the software currently runs on an IBM PC XT (or compatible computers), the results of the work done can be applied to a machine of any size. If a particular application requires a larger machine, the remaining products in the User family will enable the conversion of the data model on the micro to a fully-fledged database implementation. It has been predicted that the software would 'retail at a typical high-end PC package price'. The system has also been developed for other machines.

The growing prevalence of expert systems for micros is evident at the low-end of the machine range. Hobbyists and home-computer users will increasingly be able to diagnose car break-· downs, to evaluate human symptoms for disease, and to sex any skeletons they may come across – and all using relatively cheap micro-based facilities. We have seen the proliferation of expert systems for the IBM PC range, and other low-end suppliers have their plans. Acorn intended to make AI-related systems available for the BBC Micro, though trading difficulties may have affected the long-term strategy. Sinclair, perhaps predictably, is talking a great deal about the possibility of expert systems for the Spectrum and the QL.

Sinclair Systems

Clive Sinclair, it is reported (see, for example, Lamb, 1984), intends to move into fifth-generation computing. Such intentions will in due course yield a family of expert systems for the Sinclair computer range – as well as various speech processors, home robots and powerful microcomputers incorporating parallel processing. The wholly owned research centre, MetaLab, in Cambridge is researching new-generation integrated circuits. It is suggested, for example, that combining the processor and memory on the same chip is vital for the development of fifth-generation architectures, though the development of a parallel-architecture machine may be four or five years away.

Donald Michie, involved in the creation of the new Turing Institute in Glasgow, is designing a program for teaching micro-Prolog, an AI-related language, on the Sinclair Spectrum. One plan is for up to ten Spectrums to be linked to an IBM PC XT to train staff in rule-based programming (Michie: 'Sinclair is talking about fifth-generation projects and I have no doubt he means what he says. He has substantial resources'). At the same time some observers are aware that Sinclair has not always delivered on time.

The software company Metacomco, a division of Tenchstar Ltd, has produced a QL Lisp Development Kit, a Lisp interpreter for the Sinclair QL. Most of the development on this product was carried out by Arthur Norman and J P Fitch who worked on the Acornsoft Lisp product for the BBC Micro and Electron. This means that QL Lisp is substantially similar to the Acorn version (and QL users are likely to benefit from the Acornsoft book, *Lisp on the BBC Micro,* by Norman and Cattell – all the examples which do not use functions specific to the BBC Micro will work on the QL implementation, and all the techniques and technical details are relevant to both versions).

QL Lisp comes on microdrive, with many examples and a manual. All the built-in functions and variables are described, and an explanation of how to use the Lisp system is included. Specific BBC Micro functions can be transferred to the QL and used effectively in the new environment (there are obvious similarities between QL Lisp and Acornsoft Lisp). QL Lisp is likely to remain a front-runner Lisp facility for the QL – at least until Metacomco brings out a planned larger version. In summary (and according to the blurb), Lisp QL includes the following features:

— *full support of QL features* (eg windows, graphics and screen handling);

— *compatible with Acornsoft Lisp,* but with extra features (such as 28-bit numbers, larger work space and extra functions);

— *interpreter* (useful in program development and debugging, since changes can be rapidly tested);

— *turtle graphics* (easy-to-use graphics primitives);

— *structure editor* (for altering Lisp programs and data structures);

— *prettyprinter* (displaying Lisp programs in a suitably structured format);

— *tracer* (used during debugging to indicate the flow of control);

— *garbage collector* (required to recover any unused space);

— *28-bit integers and 250-character names* (making this version a powerful and versatile language).

A screen editor is supplied with the development kit. It is possible, using defined windows, to run multiple versions of the editor at any one time. In addition, there are facilities for horizontal and vertical scrolling, block copy and delete, file merging, automatic word wrap, etc.

There are very few working expert systems for the Sinclair range of machines. One is ZXpert, a version of Expert-Ease developed by Intelligent Terminals for the ZX Spectrum. A version of micro-Prolog has been written for Sinclair by Programming Associates, and a contract has been signed with Expert Systems Ltd (of Oxford) for the development of a version of Prolog for the QL.

Expert-Ease

This system was developed, under the direction of Donald Michie, at Edinburgh University. Launched in 1983, it was then one of the very few expert systems available for microcomputers (in this case, for the IBM PC). Expert-Ease, now available in several different versions, derived from ACLS, a minicomputer program developed using an algorithm known as Quinlan's ID3. Examples are entered (as with the Hulk program, already mentioned), whereupon the system produces the rules that apply and presents them as a decision tree. It is then possible for descriptive tags to be attached to the keywords to provide a system that can be used by non-experts. The user can build a dedicated expert system by feeding in the appropriate expertise.

ACLS (Analogue Concept Learning System) software, developed by Intelligent Terminals Ltd and supplied to Export Software International to be incorporated into a commercial package, is at the heart of Expert-Ease. The systems generated by this facility can individually involve up to 250 questions, each having up to thirty-one possible conditions or answers. A human expert enters all the questions and answers, and it is certainly possible for an incompetent expert system to be produced by an incompetent expert. The system, in effect, needs to be 'trained' to a level of expertise.

At the 1983 launch, a number of implementations (eg medical

diagnosis, farming, mechanical failure predictions, etc) were shown, and today many other implementations of Expert-Ease have been realised. Initial interest in the product was shown by such companies as Ferranti and Marconi, and after several months dozens of users – mainly companies and other organisations – had acquired versions of the system. An attractive feature of Expert-Ease was its *generalised* character, the provision of a shell that could be implemented in countless subject areas (eg for applications in finance, science, production, scheduling, engineering, administration, etc). It is represented as a new type of spreadsheet – one which (in the advertising blurb) 'helps you to solve problems, make decisions'.

The system already has some significant achievements to its credit, even finding answers to problems regarded unresolvable by other methods. For example, it enabled the US National Chess Master, Danny Kopec, to develop a complete rule-based solution to a chess end-game problem with more than 200,000 possible positions. In Ljubljana, Yugoslavia, Ivan Bratko used the system, in conjunction with colleagues, to explore aspects of lymphatic cancer. A classification was developed that proved much superior to hand-crafted schemes developed by clinicians. Then, working only with a medical student, Bratko was able to use the resulting enquiry system to equal the performance of medical experts in the diagnosis of lymphatic cancers. Other successful implementations have been achieved in the fields of information analysis, financial forecasting, anthropological research, aviation development, educational psychology, and credit control.

The advent of Expert-Ease, hailed by some observers as a major development for microcomputers, has also stimulated much critical appraisal. The product has been reviewed in many journals (see, for example, Surya, 1984; *Which Computer?*, April 1984; Naylor (i), 1984; and Crabb, 1985).

In October 1984 it was announced that Export Software International (ESI), the company set up to market Expert-Ease, had stopped trading and suspended its twenty-three employees without pay. The company's bank account was frozen in September, and soon after the ESI directors applied for voluntary liquidation. One reason for the collapse was that expected funding did not materialise. In early-1985 it was reported that Expert-Ease was to be handled by Human Edge Software in the US and by GEC Automation in the UK. Such trading events illustrate the commercial problems faced in this volatile and highly innovatory field, even by a seemingly impressive commercial product.

ES/P Advisor

Expert Systems Ltd announced ES/P Advisor, a system to enable inexperienced users to build expert systems on micros, in June 1984. One claim by the company was that this product was the first commercially available Prolog-based application package. The system is described as an expert-system shell using a concept called text animation. Relationships can be established between already recorded text data in the forms of regulations or instructions. The user needs a 16-bit micro running CP/M-86, MSDOS or PCDOS operating systems with a minimum of 128K bytes of memory.

A typical application for ES/P Advisor is where a domain consists of rules, regulations, standards or procedures that are already formally recorded in, for example, a manual or guide. The fundamental operation of the system is seen as the conditional outputting of paragraphs of text. A simple language is used to describe complex links and dependencies between paragraphs of text and the conditions under which each paragraph is relevant. The conditions are expressed in terms of the 'parameters' of the problem domain, each parameter having a value that is obtained via an interaction between the system and the user. The knowledge base has a number of sections, each of which has two parts: paragraphs of text, and a specification of each of the parameters of the problem domain. Various demonstration knowledge bases are available:

— how to do your own conveyancing to sell a registered property;

— the procedures an employer has to follow when taking on a new employee;

— how to bake bread;

— working out an opening bid in contract bridge;

— deciding if statutory sick pay is due.

Other ES/P Advisor features include links to Prolog, a disk-based knowledge base, the ability to reference parameters from within any text item that is displayed, and the ability to use full screen handling, not just scrolling, during consultation activity.

It has been emphasised that ES/P Advisor is not a general-purpose system shell. Instead it has been designed to excel in a specific type of activity, ie to exploit text animation to realise the full potential of computer applications for consultants in the office environment. The system is easy to use and, in contrast to other expert-system tools, there is little demand for the valuable time of a human expert – the required expertise is probably already recorded in a usable form. There is no facility for inexact reasoning (the blurb declares: 'Experienced expert system builders are now of the opinion that this is best avoided wherever possible, and that for many applications – such as text animation – it is not needed').

The system allows the user to change the answer to any previous question, causing a re-evaluation of decisions already made. Questions can be explained more fully, and the consultation session can be logged on a disk file. Advice can be printed as well as displayed, and the user can recap on all the advice given so far. Questions asked during a consultation depend upon earlier answers. ES/P Advisor offers a flexible consultation facility for the office environment.

Again, in common with other software packages, ES/P Advisor has been extensively reviewed in the journals (see, for example, Chang, 1984; and Naylor (ii), 1984).

MicroSYNICS

This package (called SYNICS or, with enhancements, NEBIDS) was originated by Professor Ernest Edmunds at Leicester Polytechnic. There are now various SYNICS versions. For example, there is a Fortran version being used at Unilever; Liverpool University have a BASIC version for the IBM PC; and a version for the BBC Micro is being developed.

This system is essentially designed to allow an expert or a knowledge engineer to create a user-friendly dialogue. SYNICS can provide the user with information, invite a user response, and select the next stage of the dialogue depending upon the user's response. The dialogue comprises a network of nodes, each having arcs leading to other nodes. The decision as to which arc to follow is made when the user enters a response to the question posed by the current node. In this context a node is represented by a section of displayed text, part of which is a question. The system has two basic components: the network compiler which creates a dialogue file and checks the syntax of each node and statement; and a network interpreter which runs the dialogue and controls the user interface.

SYNICS can be employed to construct expert systems that do not require inference, where a large amount of explanatory text is presented to allow the user to make a decision. The system itself makes no decisions but conducts the user to the next node in the network. It is useful as a front-end to more complex traditional programs. The Unilever implementation involves entering process-control parameters to run a chemical plant.

The NEBIDS (NEtwork-Based Interactive Dialogue System) enhancement introduces an editor and considerably enlarges the node concept. Here nodes can carry either text or graphics, which can be displayed to the user. The extension is a powerful facility but one which allows the essential simplicity of SYNICS to be preserved.

Savoir

Savoir, an expert system shell from ISI Ltd (a joint venture between Isis Systems Ltd and ICI), is available for a wide range of computers and operating systems, ranging from the IBM PC to the DEC VAX series, including the Sage 68000-based micro and PDP-11 minicomputers. A wide range of expert systems can be built by conventionally trained analysts and programmers, for subsequent use by non-specialists. ICI has used SAVOIR to create COUNSELLOR, a unique system to advise arable farmers on fungal disease control. Various features are highlighted in the promotional literature and elsewhere; for example:

— Savoir includes an easy-to-learn high-level language;

— it has a flexible interface to other programs to facilitate integration into current computer environments. Many expert systems are not easily combined with other software;

— it is the first system available with a viewdata interface to permit mass remote use via the telephone network;

— the consultation system is flexible and easy-to-understand. The system quickly displays advice without asking unnecessary questions;

— forward chaining, backward chaining and other actions are provided, and questioning is efficiently directed as soon as the system has the necessary information;

— the analyst can modify the standard Savoir messages to produce, for example, French or German versions.

The knowledge base is prepared by the knowledge engineer using a standard text editor, and it is then compiled into a form that can be used by the consultation system. The knowledge is entered using a special language that is easy to learn, and there are facilities for fuzzy-logic operations where knowledge may be uncertain. The first step is to develop an inference network that specifies the relationships between the facts and the conclusions to be drawn. This network serves as the basis of the application. Subsequent compilation checks for syntax errors and the consistency of the knowledge.

ISI also markets MicroExpert, a package suitable for developing small expert systems, for training, and for exploring the possibilities of the new technology. This package can run on a wide range of microcomputers.

MASES

This is a demonstration expert system, written in a version of Prolog and intended to run on a 64K CP/M microcomputer (see, for example, Lello, 1984). MASES (Microcomputer Advice and Selection Expert System) advises users on the selection of microcomputers from the CCTA Standard Range. It was found during design that the limitations of the CP/M microcomputer (ie speed and main memory) meant that the machine could not support the desired size of working expert system. It was therefore decided to produce a demonstration system instead. The current facility advises the user on three standard-range micros and covers a small subset of the available facilities that each machine can support.

One conclusion from the project is that a non-trivial Prolog expert system cannot be supported by a 64K microcomputer. Since expert systems often use rule-based, pattern-matching techniques, the system is too slow for effective operational use.

SUMMARY

This chapter has profiled various micro-based expert systems in the context of broad trends in artificial intelligence. Large companies – computer suppliers and others – are increasingly interested in the development of expert systems for many different purposes. Much of this interest will translate into the development of systems for low-end machines, an immense market sector.

There is no doubt that the personal-computer sector will continue to grow in the years to come. With 1985 dubbed a 'shake-out' year, there will still be massive growth in the numbers of micros sold worldwide for the rest of the decade. One prediction (in *Byte*, 1983) suggests that in 1991 around eleven million personal computers will be sold throughout the world, by which time there may be as many as 400 million personal computers in operation. Many of these machines will be powerful systems, influenced by new-generation research, programmed in Prolog (or other AI-related languages), and able to run hosts of expert systems. Personal computers will be parallel processing machines, individually based on dozens of co-operating processors, carrying several megabytes of memory, and able to work at a rate of several million instructions per second. Philip Hughes, chairman of Logica and a member of the Alvey Group, has proposed that smart applications for personal computers may be the best way for the UK to exploit the developments towards new-generation systems. The personal computer of the future will be a powerful system able to implement operations once the sole province of much larger machines. In such a context, AI-related functions, including those associated with expert systems, will be commonplace.

We are seeing the emergence of micro-based expert systems at various levels. Some – Expert-Ease, ES/P Advisor, etc – are designed specifically for low-end machines, such as the IBM PC; others, such as the micro versions of the medical system Puff, are scaled-down versions of expert systems originally designed to run on mainframes or superminis. There are similar variations, from one micro-based expert system to another, in the range of inference mechanisms employed, the size of the knowledge base, and the extent to which a system is a domain-independent shell or a dedicated implementation. Some systems have fuzzy-logic facilities to cope with uncertainties, and some do not. The full expert-systems spectrum (Chapter 3) is already immense, but even within the much more restricted microcomputer applications sector a growing proliferation of expert systems and expert-systems tools is evident.

6 Implications of Expert Systems

INTRODUCTION

The rapidly expanding expert-systems sector will have many implications for the computer industry in particular and society in general. Some of the implications are obvious, others less so. However, it is clear that many of the likely and possible consequences of expert systems have not yet been fully addressed. This chapter highlights a few of the more important implications. No lengthy discussion or evaluation is attempted. The aim is to raise topics that deserve attention in the context of a likely proliferation of economic expert systems in the years to come. These topics* will become increasingly important in the future.

THE TECHNOLOGICAL IMPACT

The development of expert systems will both affect techniques and methods in the computer industry and also provide a new spectrum of commercial products. Possible technology and applications scenarios are shown in Table 6.1. Specific focused developments will occur against general progress in computer technology – increased circuit integration, new parallel architectures, new types of user-friendly interfaces, enhanced networking facilities, etc.

There will be progress in standard ('stock') hardware and in the development of dedicated, AI-related systems (eg Lisp and Prolog machines). Low-end machines will become more powerful, increasingly able to perform functions that were once restricted to

* possibly the subject of further NCC publications.

Year	Hardware developments	Applications developments
1985	Additional manufacturers begin shipments of 36/40 bit AI workstations. Microcoded Prolog implementations running at 50 klips; first big shipments of specialised delivery vehicles.	Significant use of computer configuration and electronic equipment maintenance systems. Some major financial systems begin to show real results.
1986	Sharp fall in workstation prices begins, with move to custom LSI. Super PSI Prolog workstation delivered in Japan; running at about 250 klips.	Number of operational major systems in the USA begins sharp increase. Simpler real-time systems begin to appear – eg for process control.
1987	Compact delivery vehicles becoming available, eg for military applications. High-performance systems running at 1000 rule inferences/s, equal to 1/3 real time.	Technician systems (front-ends, diagnosis, etc) well established. Complex management and scheduling systems begin to be successful.
1988	Dataflow machines and other AI mainframes becoming available, running at several 100 MIPS. Prolog implementations at up to 1000 klips.	Real-time systems becoming established, eg for financial trading. High level creative CAD systems, eg for engineering, appearing. Sharp increase in UK major systems beginning.
1989	Parallel processors running at up to 600 MIPS. True 32-bit micros widely distributed as personal computers – well suited for office expert systems.	Major integrated management systems with proven success and increasing use. Expert systems packages established as office assistants and management aids.
1990	Military systems with dynamic adaptation, speech input, running in real time at up to 4000 rule inferences/s on 10000 rule KB.	Major systems out-performing human experts in significant areas. Real-time control of vehicles in simple environments possible. Small systems standard for many applications.

Table 6.1   Technology and Application Scenarios

expensive mainframes and minicomputers. Micros will increasingly be used as development machines but, typically, mainframes will continue to be most effective for many development projects. Micro-based systems will be important as educational tools, as demonstration systems, and for running a growing range of decision-support packages. Johnson (1984) identifies three main categories of special-purpose machines:

— special-purpose workstations, like those already available from Symbolics, Lisp Machine and Xerox;

— delivery vehicles (eg stripped-down versions of the workstations);

— 'AI mainframes' of some kind, capable of providing really powerful environments for major tasks or for time-shared access by terminals.

Government-sponsored research and company investment will influence the shape of hardware developments over the next decade. A constant theme will be the growing impact of 'new-generation', 'fifth-generation' or 'AI-related' systems.

New software will emerge both as specific development tools and commercial products. Bernard Kelly of Logica has proposed a five-level model of expert system implementation tools, ranging from the most generalised to the most specific:

— machine ('bottom') level;

— symbolic language for the system;

— 'tool-kit', building-block constructs;

— knowledge representation constructs for a domain;

— the shell, providing knowledge representation, inference and control in a standardised form.

Today there is a movement among expert-systems users from using 'home-made' shells and environments to acquiring fully-supported commercial products. As in other areas of software development, a company may develop a program for in-house use and then see the advantages of launching it as a commercial product. The initial high prices will diminish as software systems proliferate in the years to come.

Micro-based facilities will become increasingly available as educational, demonstration and applications systems. There are already, as we have seen, various Prolog implementations (eg micro-Prolog and Prolog-1) available for microcomputers, and various micro shells (eg ES/P Advisor and Apes) are written in Prolog. The number of users of micro-based expert-systems facilities is bound to increase dramatically over the next decade, though price could limit the sales of some products – whereas Logic-Based Systems is offering Apes at around £150, the M.1 facility from Teknowledge costs in the order of $12,000, both products being designed for the IBM PC. In any event, the relatively economic price of many micro-based expert systems, shells and AI-related tools will provide a route into artificial intelligence for many thousands (in due course, millions) of microcomputer users.

THE EMPLOYMENT QUESTION

The impact of technology on employment has always worried people – and often with good cause. Automation in pre-computer days affected the size and shape of the workforce, and many of the problems have been exacerbated by the spread of computer-based systems in recent years. It is easy to chart the contraction in some industry sectors as a result of computerisation and of, for example, replacing mechanical moving parts by electronic circuits:

— National Cash Register cut its manufacturing workforce from 37,000 to 18,000 between 1970 and 1975;

— American Telephone and Telegraph reduced its production workforce from 39,200 to 19,000 between 1970 and 1976;

— UK banks reduced employment from 315,600 to 263,000 between 1971 and 1976;

— Plessey (in Liverpool, UK) planned in 1984 to cut its workforce by nearly 1000;

— British Leyland has cut its workforce by 20,000, at the same time investing heavily in automation to increase worker productivity by more than 100%;

— GKN (Brymbo plant) increased steel production in 1984 by 11%, at the same time dramatically cutting the workforce.

We are familiar enough with such examples. It is likely, for example, that there is a concealed 'automation factor' in the 1984/85 coal dispute in the UK. But with the development of AI-related facilities – in particular, expert systems – the employment question takes on a new dimension.

There is already talk of how 'smart machines' will be able to dominate office work *without reference to human beings*. What has already happened in the factory environment is also likely to happen in the office workplace, and in an increasing range of service industries, often proposed as a much needed source of (human) jobs for the future. Already robot barmen serve up to thirty mixes of drinks in California, robot librarians are at work in Japanese universities, and there are experiments with robot guards in American prisons. Los Angeles has a drive-in supermarket in which an automatic 'picker' takes a computer-generated printout of the customer's order and then zooms down the warehouse corridors, under computer control, to collect the specified items. The Tokyo Institute of Technology is said to be developing a robot to perform delicate surgery on human patients; and, perhaps not unrelated to this, Imperial College (London) is developing a robot butcher to cut meat.

It has been clear for some time that middle managers are being affected, in their employment security, by automation. Thus a *Computerworld* (26 March 1984) article notes that such employees are now feeling the 'automation axe'. In this spirit, the *Guardian* (18 December 1982) was able to depict the bank manager as 'an endangered species'. Nor are the jobs in the computer industry secure from the inroads of computer-based systems. Electronic design and diagnostic engineers will increasingly find themselves outflanked by computer systems. *Computer Weekly* (3 March 1983) is able to ask, 'Is there a future for the service engineer?'.

Another key development is for computers to be able to respond intelligently when operated by computer-naive users. This means, for example, that computers will increasingly be able to write their own programs. Thus Chris Naylor (writing in *Computer Talk,* 27 February 1984) asks 'Will program generators put you out of a job?' – and what we find is that the certain types of programmer activity currently under threat is only a beginning. Ferguson (1984) begins an article with the words: 'We . . . understood the high-level objectives for application generators: to develop applications faster, *with less experienced personnel* and lower maintenance costs' (my italics). And, in the same spirit, Romberg and Thomas (1984) discuss how a computer-based expert system can be used to produce 'more reliable software in less time *with fewer people'* (my italics).

We have seen (Chapter 3) that the applications scope of expert systems is immense. In principle they can be used in any field where human intelligence is required, and increasingly such computer-based systems will be able to outperform their human counterparts. Thus a drilling expert who contributed to the knowledge base of a geological expert system noted that the system could work every day to a standard he could only manage on his best days. Starrs (1985) observes: 'The effect of developmental expert systems has so far been to enhance the work of those professionals who have encountered them, but in future *it may be that those professionals find themselves usurped by the descendants of the very systems they helped develop. Some already regard that the 'writing is on the wall''* (my italics). Similarly, Michie and Johnston (1984) point out that professionals might well be affected by the spread of expert systems: 'there are those who are sure that lawyers, for instance, specifically solicitors, could be replaced by computers and that an expert system, albeit a very big one, could actually do the job better'.

Employment policies, as framed and practised by governments and companies, are subject to human mediation. The use of computer-based systems takes on a value according to the political and socioeconomic climate. Whether human employment is threatened by expert systems is a matter for human – not yet expert-system – decision making.

THE PSYCHOLOGICAL IMPACT

The arrival of expert systems, partaking in one way or another of *intelligence,* a manifestly human attribute, may be expected to impinge on human psychology in various ways. For one thing, people are not likely to enjoy having their jobs made insecure (see above), particularly if the jobs enjoy a high status in the society. In one recorded instance (Markoff, 1983), expert-systems planners approached the circuit designers at a minicomputer company and asked them to contribute their expertise on chip design. To the evident surprise of the planners, the engineers refused to have anything to do with the project. They suspected the likely outcome if expert systems were to emerge in their own field. This anxiety is related to the broader question of how people will feel when computers are seen to be able to think like human professionals. Lee Hecht (of Teknowledge) has remarked that 'there is this unfortunate distraction that has occurred because of the use of a human analogy'. This 'distraction' is seen as adversely affecting the social and commercial acceptance of AI-related products. Moreover, inaccurate media reports 'have helped to create a distorted view of what the field is about' (quoted by Olmos, 1985).

A further psychological consequence of expert systems will be a loss of self-esteem through de-skilling. In making intelligent tasks easier to perform – with, for example, expert systems as advisors and counsellors – human beings will be discouraged from using their own competence. We have already seen this development with various classes of workers in the office environment. Office machines have been promoted as usable 'by anyone, however small their IQ' (Parks, 1980), and salesmen have claimed that anyone can use the new systems ('even the silliest girl in your typing pool'). A CEGB supervisor, following the introduction of word processors, declared that 'a less experienced typist is able to produce the same quality of work as a really skilled girl and about as quickly'. What is true of word processors is equally true of many other computer-based facilities, including expert systems. The aim is to make the task easy for the human user. There is an effective transfer of intelligent activity from the person to the machine. This developing trend will have inevitable consequences for human psychology.

It has frequently been asserted that computers 'dehumanise' their users in various ways, a view associated with such writers as Illich (1975) and Weizenbaum (1976). There is in fact a body of research work (eg Orcutt and Anderson, 1977) that suggests that computers have various detrimental effects on human psychology: people, it seems, are variously rendered less social, less content with their self-image, and less able to communicate in effective ways (modes of communication may be 'scaled down' to accord with what a computer, rather than a person, might expect). A spectrum of dehumanising effects can be charted, though many of these are supported by little more than anecdotal evidence. Again we may speculate on how conversational expert systems are likely to impinge on human sociability and communication modes.

In addition to the psychological impact of expert systems on *users,* there will also be growing psychological effects on *developers* of AI-related products. For example, B Whitby (in Yazdani and Narayanan, eds, 1984) can comment that 'the economic pressures which are today shaping the AI paradigm are likely to render it progressively more elitist'. The need for security and specialisation will increase as commercial success depends increasingly on companies being able to keep their progress out of the hands of market competitors. And the increased use of military expert systems will put a further premium on the need for security. In such circumstances, we may expect designers and developers to become increasingly secretive, elitist, and indifferent to broader social considerations.

All the supposed adverse effects of increased computerisation in general and the anticipated proliferation of expert systems in particular are open to debate. The advent of systems that may be deemed, in some sense, intelligent and moreover a threat to a wide spectrum of professional activity may be expected to affect human psychology in many ways. This is a topic that has scarcely been considered in any depth but it is certain to affect the general acceptance – and so commercial viability – of AI-related products in the future.

DO YOU BELIEVE THE SYSTEM?

A common feature of expert systems is that they are able to explain their reasoning to a human user. If, for example, a system produces what may seem to be an extraordinary or incredible conclusion, the user may want to know how it was achieved. This possibility is likely to become increasingly real as expert systems become more competent. Various observers (eg Michie, 1980) have pointed out that expert systems sometimes find solutions to problems in ways that are opaque to human observers. In such circumstances there is a pressing need for the system to be able to provide information to help the human observer to understand the situation. The provision of 'windows' for this purpose may be taken as a primary design requirement in expert systems. However, even where effective 'windows' are provided, there may still be grounds for concern.

We are well aware of the *authority* of computer systems: computer printout or a comprehensive display is, it seems, already sanctified. If a user has, in all diligence, repeatedly checked expert-system conclusions and been satisfied by the explanations, he may be less inclined to check in future: conclusions will tend to be accepted 'on the nod'. Here, there will be a progressive transfer of decision-making responsibility from the human user to the machine. It is one thing to have an available window, quite another to use it systematically in *all* appropriate circumstances.

This highlights one aspect of the relationship between human users and AI-related systems. If the systems are seen as competent they will be acquired and used, and in due course their deliverances – in the fields of medicine, government planning, financial-policy making, military-strategy formulation, etc – may be accepted too readily. This aspect, in common with other areas of expert-systems usage, deserves to be considered in some detail.

WHO IS LIABLE?

Another central concern is the question of *liability* when expert systems are involved in decision making. Put another way, who is responsible if an expert system gives bad advice – the programmer, the supplier, the user, or the system itself? What a field for American-style litigation! If a physician makes a wrong diagnosis there may well be legal, as well as medical, consequences. But who is to be prosecuted if a medical expert system makes a wrong and harmful diagnosis? (The question of liability is discussed in various contributions to Yazdani and Narayanan, eds, 1984.)

The difficulties in this area become apparent when one considers the various steps that go into generating an expert system. A specialist's expertise is collected and expressed – say, in heuristics – by the knowledge engineer, whereupon the findings are presented to a programmer for coding the system. But did the specialist agree the heuristics? And was the translation of heuristics to code 100% accurate? How well did the expert express his expertise? Is the knowledge engineer, as a non-expert in the domain, in a position to judge? And what is the value of the supplier's disclaimer at the start of the program run? Did the user use the system properly, noting any caveats that might have been made by the expert or the supplier? If something goes wrong – in, for example, a critical medical area – who is to blame? Should pieces of software be made honorary members of the British Medical Association or the Law Society?

Narayanan and Perrott (in Yazdani and Narayanan, eds, 1984) ask whether a computer can have legal rights, and other writers have begun to explore the question of 'computer criminality'. It is even possible to explore existing legal categories to see how established legislation can illuminate the question of computer liability. For example, is it arguable that a computer has the legal status of a child, an animal, a slave or an agency (as with the law of agency). Already there is a growing literature on such topics, though no consensual conclusions. Sometimes the debate is immensely important – when, for instance, it focuses on the launching of nuclear warheads (Anderson, 1984).

Clifford Johnson, now of Stanford University, aimed to prove in court that the development of sophisticated computer systems to control the launch of nuclear missiles violates the American constitution. It is argued that it is unconstitutional to abrogate political power to a machine. There are already signs that the US, under the terms of the Strategic Computing Initiative, is aiming to build supercomputers and AI facilities to provide a 'launch on warning' capability, where a missile-launch decision could be taken without human involvement.

If computers are eventually granted human-like powers of

judgement and decision making, it may seem rational to hold them responsible for their actions. But how could anyone sue a computer for damages? Or vote it out of office following a calamitous term of service to the community?

WHOSE EXPERTISE?

Many of the liability considerations (see above) relate to the quality of the expertise stored in the knowledge base of the expert system. In much of the literature dealing with the design of expert systems, there appears to be an assumption that the specialist's knowledge is complete and objective, if only he will oblige by divulging it. In fact, experts vary not only in their general level of competence but also in the extent to which their knowledge is framed within a value system. Apart from being more or less competent, human experts can vary in their moral or ideological postures, and this fact becomes increasingly important with expert systems relating to financial policy making, political problem solving and military strategy. Suppose, for instance, you require an expert system to deal with economics. Whose expertise do you mine? That of a Keynesian or a monetarist? Does a change of government mean that half the operational expert systems have to be scrapped? Or should they be flexible enough to adapt, as advisory civil servants are supposed to do? And what of strategic military expert systems – do they operate according to 'better Red than dead' or 'better dead than Red'? There could be alarming practical consequences for human society, according to which (implicit or explicit) values are written into expert systems in key areas that affect human life.

This means that we should be wary of the limitations of expert systems, in the full knowledge that limitations will exist irrespective of machine processing power, storage capacity or the sophistication of a symbolic processing language. At present, system expertise has to derive from human experts – who are all, to some extent, forgetful, inconsistent and prejudiced.

THE DOMESTIC DANGERS

It should now be apparent what the domestic dangers are likely to be in the context of a proliferation of expert systems for low-end machines. One can think of various circumstances in which the ordinary home computer user might run into problems using expert systems as problem-solving or decision-making tools. The following are a few of the possibilities:

—   an erroneous medical diagnosis may be given for, say, a child, leading to a delay in proper medical attention;
—   inadequate tax advice may be provided, following neglect of an unusual individual circumstance, leading the user into trouble with the tax authorities;
—   the user may be wrongly advised to invest money in an enterprise, or to buy an unsuitable item.

Even if the system is equipped with an 'explanation window', the user may be unable or unwilling to use it. The 'explanation' may be beyond his grasp. And it may also be true that the micro-based expert system, with its evident limitations, may lack the flexibility or the knowledge to cope with changes in medical practice (eg availability of drugs), new legislation, and changes in the financial or market scene (eg fluctuations in the exchange rate, new share flotations, etc). It is likely that the limitations of expert systems in general will prove to be writ large where micro-based systems are concerned. One consequence is that the domestic user, possibly the most inclined to trust the deliverances of clever low-end systems, is the most at risk.

SUMMARY

This chapter has briefly profiled some obvious implications of the increased use of expert systems. Some of the implications are akin to those of increased computerisation in general, whereas others relate specifically to the growing spectrum of AI products. The topics raised – employment, the psychological impact, system reliability, system liability, domestic hazards, etc – deserve to be considered in detail. It will be found that these topics will lead to other questions, many of which are overlapping and hard to resolve. But if expert systems are intended to benefit people in society, rather than simply serving as a new commercial sector, then it is important that the questions are addressed. They will become more pressing as expert systems, increasingly available for microcomputers, become commonplace throughout the developed world.

APPENDIX 1

References and Bibliography

CHAPTER 1

Anderson I, AI is stark naked from the ankles up, *New Scientist*, 15 November 1984, pp 18-21

Bartimo J, Aiming for the executive suite, Software offers to help companies make decisions, *InfoWorld*, 19 November 1984, pp 30-33

Bergheim K, Counselling by computer, *InfoWorld*, 29 October 1984, p 21

Bidmead C, Brainstorm, *Practical Computing*, July 1984, pp 80-81

Black G, Searle stirs up talk about thinking, *Computer Weekly*, 29 November 1984, p 21

Braybrooke P and Schofield J, The Sales Edge, *Practical Computing*, May 1984, p 47

Caruso D, Software probes the mind, *InfoWorld*, 24 September 1984, pp 34-35, 38-39

Coleman D, Decision support systems, *Data Processing*, October 1984, pp 35-36

Direct brain entry possible by 1990, *Computer Management*, November 1984, p 9

Durham T, Fifth-generation fever, *Practical Computing*, October 1984, pp 115-117

Feigenbaum E A and McCorduck P, *The Fifth Generation*, Michael Joseph, 1984

Freyenfeld W A, *Decision Support Systems*, NCC Publications, 1984

Garner R, Japanese reveal inference software, *Computing*, 15 November 1984, p 3

GLEB cash boosts GP's expert systems, *Datalink*, 11 June 1984

Green-Armytage J, The IT roll call, *Computer Weekly*, 6 December 1984, p 31

Haner J, Mindware, spreadsheets for ideas, *Computerworld*, 29 October 1984, pp ID/7-ID/8, ID/12

Highberger D and Edson D, Intelligent computing era takes off, *Computer Design*, September 1984, pp 79-95

Hofstadter D R and Dennett D C (eds), *The Mind's I*, Penguin Books, 1982

Johnson T, *The Commercial Application of Expert Systems Technology*, Ovum Ltd, 1984

Jones R, Enter the electronic advisor, *Computing*, 1 November 1984, pp 12-13

Lamb J, Peace and love in the computer jungle, *New Scientist*, 22 November 1984

Madden D, Benefits stay mainly elusive, *Computer Weekly*, 6 December 1984, p 23

Malik R, Operator, I want a person to person call – in Japanese, *Computer News*, 1 November 1984, p 32

Marquet J, The trouble with AI, *Computerworld*, 19 October 1984, p 10

Martins G R, The overselling of expert systems, *Datamation*, 1 November 1984, pp 76, 78, 80

McLening M, A solution looking for a problem?, *Software*, June 1984, pp 12-14

Mill J, Giants battle to win market victory, *Computing*, 1 November 1984, pp 10-11

Moody G, From accounts to Apricots, *Practical Computing*, November 1984, pp 80-81

Murtha T, Bringing AI home, *Datamation*, 1 January 1985, pp 34-36

Neimark J, Psych-out software, *Datamation*, 15 October 1984, pp 32-34, 37, 40

Quinn E, US firms step up joint AI research fund, *Computing*, 11 October 1984, p 18

Sanders J, Brainstorm, *Personal Computer World*, January 1984, pp 151-155

Schatz W and Verity J W, Weighing DARPA's AI plans, *Datamation*, 1 August 1984, pp 34, 39, 42-43

Simons G L, *Towards Fifth-Generation Computers*, NCC Publications, 1983

Simons G L, *Introducing Artificial Intelligence*, NCC Publications, 1984

Smith K, UK accents voice gear, *Electronics Week*, 19 November 1984, pp 32-33

Sullivan K, Long-term research key to quest for next generation, *Computerworld*, 22 October 1984, p 30

Valid AI definition lost amid industry jargon, *Computerworld*, 26 November 1984, p 28

Warren C, Decision-support program boosts AI techniques, *Mini-Micro Systems*, December 1984, p 30

Watt P, Artificial intelligence myths, *InfoWorld*, 18 June 1984, pp 46-47

White P, Where research money is going, *Computer Weekly*, 6 December 1984, p 25

Winston P H and Prendergast K A (eds), *The AI Business*, MIT Press, 1984

CHAPTER 2

Anderson J, Prediction and Predilection: Creative Computing and the future of the micro industry, *Creative Computing,* November 1984, pp 51-52, 56, 60, 62

Arthur C, Economists see a micro explosion, *Computer Weekly,* 15 November 1984, p 16

Ash N, Programs that write programs, *Practical Computing,* June 1983, pp 138-142

Atkin G, The multi-purpose micro marches ahead, *Engineering Computers,* November 1984, pp 66-67, 69

Barron I, Cavill P, May D and Wilson P, Transputer does 5 or more MIPS even when not used in parallel, *Electronics,* 17 November 1983, pp 109-115

Bender E, Small change, *Computerworld*, 31 December 1984/7 January 1985, pp 32, 34-35, 37

Blakeney S, Around the world in 16K, *Computerworld,* 31 December 1984/7 January 1985

Bond G, CLOUT and SALVO, *Byte,* October 1984, pp 279-287

Bond J, Circuit density and speed boost tomorrow's hardware, *Computer Design,* September 1984, pp 210-225

Bores L D, AGAT, A Soviet Apple II computer, *Byte,* November 1984, pp 135-136, 486, 488, 490

Burstein D, Singapore's 21st century dream, *Datamation,* 15 October 1984, pp 155-156, 158

Chard A, *Evaluating Program Generators for Micros*, NCC Publications, 1985

Cote A J, Speech images on the IBM PC, *Byte,* November 1983, pp 402-407

Crosbie R E, ISIM, A continuous-system simulation language, *Byte,* May 1984, pp 400-403

Data base program bows for IBM micros, *Computerworld,* 19 November 1984, p 59

Duffin P and Lello S F, MASES – a PROLOG expert system, *Information Age,* October 1984, pp 210-219

Durham T, Expert systems join in fight against cancer, *Computing,* 11 October 1984, pp 26-27

Gallagher R T, Expert system uses AI for natural sound, *Electronics Week,* 7 January 1985, p 19

Garner R, NEC designs ai cad system, *Computing,* 15 November 1984, p8

Gottinger H W, Hazard: an expert system for screening environmental chemicals on carcinogenity, *Expert Systems,* Vol. 1, No. 2, 1984, pp 169-176

Hartley R T, CRIB: computer fault-finding through knowledge engineering, *Computer,* March 1984, pp 76-83

Hertz D B, Artificial intelligence and the business manager, *Computerworld,* 24 October 1983, pp ID/21-ID/26

Ishizuka M, Japanese work in expert systems, *Expert Systems,* Vol. 1, No. 1, 1984, pp 51-56

Johnson T, *The Commercial Application of Expert Systems Technology,* Ovum Ltd, 1984

Johnston R, Intelligent robots find their feet, *Computer Weekly,* 6 December 1984, p 33

Jones F N and Watson P A, Expert systems and the telecom manager, *Telecommunications,* September 1984, pp 61-1, 70-1, 77-1, 82-1, 90-1

Lineback J R, AI transforms CAD/CAM to CIM, *Electronics Week,* 17 December 1984, pp 17-18

Michaelsen R H, An expert system for federal tax planning, *Expert Systems,* Vol. 1, No. 2, 1984, pp 149-167

Michaelsen R and Michie D, Expert systems in business, *Datamation,* November 1983, pp 240-246

Narendra K S and Mars P, The use of learning algorithms in telephone traffic routing – a methodology, *Automatica,* Vol. 19, No. 5, 1983, pp 495-502

Pratt C A, An artificially intelligent locomotive mechanic, *Simulation*, January 1984, pp 40-41

Ritter M, Computers handle algebra, too, *Simulation*, July 1984, pp 49-50

Rogers W et al, Computer-aided medical diagnosis: literature review, *International Journal of Biomedical Computing*, 10, 1979, pp 267-289

Schindler M, Artificial intelligence begins to pay off with expert systems for engineering, *Electronic Design*, 9 August 1984, pp 106-146

Scott P, Expert system rates software, *Computerworld (Australia)*, 7 December 1984, pp 1, 16

Sedlmeyer R L et al, Knowledge-based fault localisation in debugging, *The Journal of Systems and Software*, December 1983, pp 301-307

Sell P S, Expert systems are here, now, *Data Processing*, March 1984, pp 28-29

Shaw S, Heard on the hill, AI emerges from the shadows, *Mini-Micro Systems*, November 1983, p 51

Simmons M K, Artificial intelligence for engineering design, *Computer-Aided Engineering Journal*, April 1984, pp 75-83

Smith M F and Bowen J A, Knowledge and experience-based systems for analysis and design of microprocessor applications hardware, *Microprocessors and Microsystems*, December 1982, pp 515-518

Stefik M J and de Kleer J, Prospects for expert systems in CAD, *Computer Design*, 21 April 1983, pp 65-76

Sullivan K, Financial industry fertile ground for expert systems, *Computerworld*, 22 October 1984, p 29

Thomas D E et al, Automatic data path synthesis, *Computer*, December 1983, pp 59-70

Waterman D A and Peterson M A, Evaluating civil claims: an expert systems approach, *Expert Systems*, July 1984, pp 65-76

Webster R, Expert systems, *Personal Computer World,* January 1983, pp 118-119

Wilkins B, AI techniques considered for DBMS use, *Computerworld,* 3 December 1984, p 57

Zivy G M, The role of expert systems in producing log interpretation software, *Expert Systems,* Vol. 1, No. 1, 1984, p 57-62

CHAPTER 4

Addis T R, Expert systems: an evolution in information retrieval, *Information Technology: Research and Development,* 1, 1982, pp 301-324

Alty J L and Coombs M J, *Expert Systems – Concepts and Examples,* NCC Publications, 1984

Benzon B, The visual mind and the Macintosh, *Byte,* January 1985, pp 113-114, 116, 118, 120, 122, 124, 128, 130

Bidmead C, Food for thought, *Practical Computing,* October 1984, pp 128-130

Blake A, Ways of seeing, *Practical Computing,* October 1984, p 127

Campbell J A, Expert systems, *IUCC Bulletin,* Vol. 5, 1983, pp 63-67

Cox I J, Expert systems, *Electronics & Power,* March 1984, pp 237-240

Dahl V, Logic programming as a representation of knowledge, *Computer,* October 1983, pp 106-111

d'Agapeyeff A, *Expert Systems,* NCC Publications, 1983

d'Ambrosio B, Expert systems, myth or reality?, *Byte,* January 1985, pp 275-282

Durham T, Keeping the machine on a tight leash at all times, *Computing,* 13 December 1984, pp 26-27

Eden C, Smithin T and Wiltshire J, Cognition simulation and learning, *Journal of Experiential Learning and Simulation,* 2, 1980, pp 131-143

Expert systems, *Which Computer?*, April 1984, pp 58-64

Feigenbaum E A and McCorduck P, *The Fifth Generation,* Michael Joseph, 1984

Foremski T, Extracting experts' expertise, *Computing,* 25 October 1984, pp 12-13

Foster E, Artificial intelligence faces a crossroads, *Mini-Micro Systems,* May 1984, pp 119-125

Goldes H J, Designing the human-computer interface, *Educational Technology,* October 1983, pp 9-15

Goodall A, Logic programming in Prolog, *Data Processing,* March 1984, pp 37-39, 48

Hindin H J, Fifth-generation computing: dedicated software is the key, *Computer Design,* September 1984, pp 150-164

Israel D J, The role of logic in knowledge representation, *Computer,* October 1983, pp 37-41

Jain R and Haynes S, Imprecision in computer vision, *Computer,* August 1982, pp 39-47

James M, *Artificial Intelligence in BASIC,* Newnes Microcomputer Books, 1984

Johnson T, *The Commercial Application of Expert Systems Technology,* Ovum Ltd, 1984

King T, Expert systems with 68000 and LISP, *Microprocessors and Microsystems,* September 1984, pp 374-376

Kinnucan P, Computers that think like experts, *High Technology,* January 1984

Kowalski R, AI and software engineering, *Datamation,* 1 November 1984, pp 92-102

Lee G, Lelouche R, Meissonnier V, Ornato M, Zarri G and Zarri-Baldi L, Artificial intelligence, history and knowledge representation, *Computers and the Humanities,* 16, 1982, pp 25-34

Lenat D B, The ubiquity of discovery, *Journal of Artificial Intelligence*, 9, 1977, pp 257-286

Mace S, Can natural language sell?, *InfoWorld*, 12 November 1984, pp 36-41

Marcus R S, An experimental comparison of the effectiveness of computers and humans as search intermediaries, *Journal of the American Society for Information Science, 34*, 6, 1983, pp 381-404

McDermott J, To think for themselves, computers must first learn some common sense, *Electronic Design*, 31 October 1984, pp 83-84

Michie D, Automating the synthesis of expert knowledge, *Aslib Proceedings, 36*, 9, September 1984, pp 337-343

Microsoft launches Lisp for PCs, *Expert Systems, 1*, 2, 1984, pp 108-109

Mokhoff N, Artificial intelligence systems make their mark, *Computer Design*, November 1983, pp 33-36

Naylor C, Build Your Own Expert System, *Sigma Technical Press*, 1983

Naylor C, Tongue-tied, *Practical Computing*, October 1984, p 125

Pountain D, Prolog on microcomputers, *Byte*, December 1984, pp 355-362

Ramsay A, The POPLOG program development system, *Microprocessors and Microsystems*, September 1984, pp 368-373

Riley J, Minis pinch extra ground, *Computer Weekly*, 8 November 1984, pp 38, 40, 44

Sagalowicz D, Development of an expert system, *Expert Systems, 1*, 2, 1984, pp 137-141

Shaket E, Fuzzy semantics for a natural-like language defined over a world of blocks, *Artificial Intelligence Memo 4*, University of California, 1976

Simons G L, *Introducing Artificial Intelligence*, NCC Publications, 1984

Sloman A, Hardy S and Gibson J, POPLOG: a multilanguage program development environment, *Information Technology: Research and Development,* 2, 1983, pp 109-122

Stefik M, Aikins J, Balzer R, Beniot J, Birnbaum L, Hayes-Roth F and Sacerdoti E, *The Organization of Expert Systems: A Prescriptive Tutorial,* Research Report VLSI-82-1, XEROX PARC, Palo Alto, CA, 1982

Stevens M, Mind over matter, *Personal Computer World,* October 1984, pp 136-138

Valiant L G, A theory of the learnable, *Communications of the ACM,* November 1984, pp 1134-1142

Walton P, Prolog to the fifth generation, *Infomatics,* December 1984, pp 53-55

Webber B L, Logic and natural language, *Computer,* October 1983, pp 43-46

Wess B P, Artificial intelligence techniques speed software development, *Mini-Micro Systems,* September 1984, pp 127-136

Zadeh L A, Fuzzy sets, *Information and Control,* 8, 1965, pp 338-353

Zadeh L A, Commonsense knowledge representation based on fuzzy logic, *Computer,* October 1983, pp 61-65

CHAPTER 5

Artificial intelligence faces up to the challenges of the real world, *Electronic Design,* 26 July 1984, pp 63-64

Beechhold H F, Expert Choice, *InfoWorld,* 28 January 1985, pp 45-48

Berney K, Experts write own programs, *Electronics Week,* 22 October 1984, pp 29-30

Chang P, Expert advice, *Personal Computer World,* 1984, pp 150-151

Corley C J and Statz J A, Lisp workstation brings AI power to a user's desk, *Computer Design,* January 1985, pp 155-162

Crabb D, Expert-Ease, *Infoworld,* 28 January 1985, pp 4

Creeger M, Lisp machines come out of the lab, *Computer Design,* November 1983, pp 207-208, 210, 212, 214-216

Durham T, Talking at the speed of Lisp, *Computing,* 1 November 1984, pp 26-27

Evanczuk S and Manuel T, Practical systems use natural languages and store human expertise, *Electronics,* 1 December 1983, pp 139-145

Expert-Ease, *Which Computer?,* April 1984, pp 68, 70-71

Fawcett S, Breaking the expert systems bottleneck, *Computing,* 12 April 1984, pp 26-27

Foster E S, Two firms aim Lisp AI systems at commercial market, *Mini-Micro Systems,* October 1983, pp 62, 65, 68

Goering R, Do-it-yourself development tools speed AI applications, *Computer Design,* December 1984, pp 29-39

Hindin H J, Revolution brewing in workstation technology, *Computer Design,* January 1985, pp 111-124

Huggins T, AI systems made simple, *Infomatics,* January 1985, pp 11-12

Johnson T, *The Commercial Application of Expert Systems Technology,* Ovum Ltd, 1984

Konopasek M and Jayaraman S, Expert systems for personal computers, *Byte,* May 1984, pp 137-138, 140, 144, 146, 150, 152, 154, 156

Lamb J, Sinclair goes AI, *Datamation,* 15 October 1984, pp 67, 70, 75

Lello S F, MASES: a demonstration expert system, *CCTA News,* January 1984, pp 21-22

Mace S, Expert-Ease creates expert systems on IBM PC, *Infoworld,* 19 March 1984, pp 11-12

Manuel T, Lisp and Prolog machines are proliferating, *Electronics,* 3 November 1983, pp 132-137

Mason L, 'World first' in expert systems, *Computerworld (Australia)*, 19 October 1984, pp 1, 12

Mill J, Expert-Ease firm seeks distributor, *Computing*, 15 November 1984, p 11

Mokhoff N, Artificial intelligence concepts are being put to practical use, *Computer Design*, 15 October 1984, pp 42, 44-46

Naylor C (i), Expert-Ease lays down ground rules for an expert decision, *Software*, April 1984, pp 34-35

Naylor C (ii), ES/P Advisor, *Practical Computing*, October 1984, pp 120-121

Naylor C (iii), Discriminating experts, *Practical Computing*, March 1984, pp 108-112

Rand M, Sperry maps push into AI, *Electronics Week*, 12 November 1984, pp 34, 36

Reed K, ICL offers knowledge-based 'shell', *Computerworld*, 16 November 1984, p 4

Rose C D, Investment shifts into AI, *Electronics Week*, 4 February 1985, pp 28-30

Savoir: expert systems meet the videotex mass-market, *Expert Systems*, Vol. 1, No. 2, pp 105-106

Sheil B, Family of personal Lisp machines speed AI program development, *Electronics*, 3 November 1983, pp 153-156

Simons G L, *Towards Fifth-Generation Computers*, NCC Publications, 1983

Spitznogle F, Practical tools earn AI new level of respectability, *Computer Design*, September 1984, pp 197-200

Surya, Expert-Ease, *Personal Computer World*, June 1984, pp 208-213

Tate P, The blossoming of European AI, *Datamation*, 1 November 1984, pp 85-86, 88

Verity J W, AI tools arrive in force, *Datamation*, 15 September 1984, pp 44, 46, 50, 53

CHAPTER 6

Anderson I, Can computers legally launch warheads?, *New Scientist,* 25 October 1984, p 7

Beekman G, Do you believe that 'expert'?, *Info World,* 28 January 1985, p 8

Computers that learn could lead to disaster, *New Scientist,* 17 January 1980, p 160

Curnow H J, Artificial intelligence – a survey, *Information Age,* January 1985, pp 10-14

Ferguson G T, A letter from users to vendors of application generators, *Computerworld,* 26 March 1984

Hamilton R, Who's responsible for uses of AI?, *Computer Talk,* 19 March 1984

Illich I, *Medical Nemesis: The Expropriation of Health,* Calder and Boyars, 1975

Johnson T, *The Commercial Application of Expert Systems Technology,* Ovum Ltd, 1984

Kowalski R, Applying the rules to both human beings and machines, *Computing,* 13 December 1984, p 35

Manuel T and Rand M B, Has AI's time come at last?, *Electronics Week,* 4 February 1985, pp 51-62

Markoff J, Computers that think, *Info World,* 25 July 1983

Michie D, P-KP4; expert system to human being conceptual checkmate of dark ingenuity, *Computing,* 17 July 1980

Michie D and Johnston R, *The Creative Computer,* Viking, 1984

Mueller R E and Mueller E T, Would an intelligent computer have a 'right to life'?, *Creative Computing,* August 1983, pp 149-153

Narayanan A, Ascribing mental predicates to computers, *Research Report* R-102, Department of Computer Science, University of Exeter, 1981

Narayanan A, What is it like to be a machine?, *Research Report* R-116, Department of Computer Science, University of Exeter, 1983

Olmos D, AI field faces crucial barriers to acceptance, *Computerworld,* 31 December 1984/7 January 1985, pp 129, 134

Orcutt J D and Anderson R E, Social interaction, dehumanisation and the 'computerised other', *Sociology and Social Research,* 61, 1977, pp 380-397

Parks T H, How to be run off one's feet in a more up-to-date electronic fashion, *Guardian,* 19 November 1980

Roberts S, Artificial intelligence, *Mini-Micro Systems,* December 1983, pp 229-233

Romberg F A and Thomas A B, Reusable code, reliable software, *Computerworld,* 26 March 1984

Starrs A M, Expert systems – their uses and possible impact upon society, *Electronics & Power,* January 1985, pp 37-41

Weizenbaum J, *Computer Power and Human Reason,* W H Freeman, San Francisco, 1976

Yazdani M and Narayanan A (eds), *Artificial Intelligence: Human Effects,* Ellis Horwood, 1984

APPENDIX 2

Summary of Alvey Report

THE ALVEY REPORT

The Alvey Report (about 80 pages long) was published in September/October 1982 as a direct response to Japanese fifth-generation plans. (The various Japanese programmes are seen as 'a major competitive threat'.) The Report identifies four key technical areas in which major advances are required for the implementation of an Advanced Information Technology (AIT) programme:

— software engineering;

— man/machine interface (MMI);

— intelligent knowledge-based systems (IKBS);

— very large-scale integration (VLSI).

In the *Executive Summary* (Section 2), specific practical measures are proposed for the development of information technology in Britain. These recommendations include:

— investment of £350 million over five years, with Government providing three-quarters of the cost and industry providing the remainder (and also the 'much larger sums needed to translate the results of the programme into marketable products');

— collaborative effort between industry, the academic sector and other research organisations to get the best value from Government support;

— investment by Government of £57 million to support research and training in academic institutions, with dissemination of results 90 per cent funded by Government;

— an effective doubling of UK effort in the four enabling technologies: software engineering, MMI, IKBS and VLSI;

— participation of foreign multinationals in the UK effort, only where they can contribute a particular asset, where their involvement will benefit UK industry as a whole, and where it is guaranteed that valuable technical information will not leak from the UK;

— establishment of a new Directorate, within the Department of Industry, charged with implementing the programme. SERC and the Ministry of Defence should also be involved in the control of the programme and should provide some of the Government funding;

— early initiation of the programme.

The Case for the Programme (Section 3) is argued on the basis of five main propositions:

— on current trends, the UK share of the growing world IT market will diminish;

— to reverse these trends, it is necessary to have competitive levels of achievement in certain fundamental enabling technologies;

— the enabling technologies can be identified;

— a strong domestic capability in these technologies is required ('we cannot depend upon other countries supplying them');

— the necessary national collaborative effort requires Government backing.

Individual companies will be expected to exploit the results of the programme (whether or not they have been involved in its implementation), applying commercial judgments on market opportunities. It is emphasised that the level of Government support will render the results of the programme public property 'which can be made generally available for exploitation by British industry'. The potentially stimulating effect of the programme on small companies is seen as one of its major attractions. The proposed UK programme is represented as independent of the current ESPRIT proposals from the European Commission, though a collaborative UK programme 'would assist in feeding in the UK input to any EEC programme'. The French, for example, have embarked upon their own national IT programme, independent of Esprit.

Section 4 *(Technical Content and Targets)* explores an approach to the four identified enabling technologies: software engineering, MMI, IKBS and VLSI. It is suggested that a communication network be established to connect the organisations that will need to cooperate in developing these inter-dependent technologies. The importance, for software engineering, of developing Information Systems Factories (ISFs) is emphasised, and a development strategy for each of the enabling technologies is described in some detail (Section 4, occupying 38 pages, represents about half of the total report). Specific topics are discussed and development timescales are defined.

In Section 5 *(Cost and Funding),* the proposed distribution of Government funding over the various elements in the programme (software engineering, VLSI, CAD, MMI, IKBS, communications, demonstrators and education) is tabulated for a five-year period (total cost: £352 million). It is expected that Government will fund the major share of the programme but that industry will need to raise 'the much larger funds needed to translate the results of the programme into marketable products'. Proposed academic investment (total: £56 million) is also shown distributed over the various programme elements.

Section 6 *(Management of the Programme)* explores the character of the proposed Directorate. A Director, with proper authority within the Department of Industry, will report to a Board which would serve as a steering committee. Assistant Directors are envisaged who would need to be expert authorities in their respective technical areas. The main task of the Directorate would be to ensure that the programme was effectively implemented, its targets met to the agreed timescale. It will award contracts, monitor projects, disseminate programme results, explore the question of Industrial Property Rights (IPR), etc.

Section 7 *(Human Resources)* explores the provision of the skilled manpower essential to the implementation of the programme. The Directorate will monitor the manpower requirements and, by means of recruitment and training, ensure that they are met. It is emphasised that the need to train personnel varies from one technical sector to another: there are, for example, few active participants in the UK in the IKBS area, though Britain has an excellent reputation for research in computer science. An IT Fellowship, a dispersed national institute, is proposed as a means of exploiting existing expertise. Action is also recommended in schools and other educational organisations.

Section 8 *(Summary of Recommendations)* lists proposals as ten discrete paragraphs. These identify such requirements as: the need for a national, Government-backed, collaborative effort; research in the enabling technologies; proportions of government and industry funding; identification of property rights; the need for a Directorate; and the timescale of the programme. It is concluded that 'the programme should be implemented immediately to safeguard the future competitiveness of the UK IT industry'.

APPENDIX 3

Glossary

Algorithm

A set of rules or defined process which performs a particular task; a mathematical formula or program procedure

Alphanumeric

A group of characters which includes a mix of numerals, alphabetic letters and (sometimes) punctuation marks and other symbols

Analogue

A way of representing numerical values by a continuously changing physical quantity; for example the hands of a non-digital watch or sound-level display on a hi-fi set

Application

The user task performed by a computer (such as playing a game, making an airline reservation or processing a company's accounts)

Architecture

1. The blueprint design which defines how the components within a computer system are interrelated. 2. The internal structure of a computer, such as the number of bits in the basic word length and the instruction set specification. 3. The design of computing elements and information flows in a network

Arithmetic and logic unit

The part of a computer where arithmetic and logical operations take place using accumulators and special circuits. Sometimes referred to as the Arithmetic Unit

Array

An ordered group of information elements, such as a list or table. Each element is identified by a subscript which specifies its relative position within the array. An array can have any number of dimensions

Artificial Intelligence (AI)

The study of how computing can be applied to perform tasks that involve intellectual, communications and sensory activities akin to those in human beings

Assembler

1. Software to translate a low-level language program into machine-readable code. 2. An assembly language

Assembly language

A low-level programming language, similar in structure to machine code but using mnemonic instructions and symbolic addressing

Back-up

1. Doubling up on systems components to improve availability, with the stand-by moving into action if its twinned element fails. 2. Information held separately from current data which can be used to reconstitute the information base to a recent state, if the current data is corrupted or destroyed. 3. A computer installation which could be used to run work normally processed on another computer that is out of action for some reason

Desk-top system	A complete computer small enough to fit on an office desk
Digital	Representation of information by discrete numerical quantities
Direct Numerical Control	NC and other machine tools controlled by a central computer
Disk	See Magnetic disk
Distributed processing	A system or network where computing capabilities are in many locations rather than at a central point; also known as distributed computing or distributed data processing
Domain (expert)	A domain, or knowledge domain, is a specific area of expertise to be treated by an expert system. A domain expert is the person whose expertise is to be coded into the expert system
Dumb terminal	A terminal which does not incorporate any of its own computing capability and can operate only when linked on-line to a computer
Duplex	A communications link which allows transmission in two directions simultaneously (see Half-duplex)
Electronic mail	The transmission of messages, documents and other information by electronic means, such as via the telephone and by linked communicating word processors
Electronic office	General term to encompass future office procedures and jobs where a variety of computer-based systems and electronic devices are used

End user
A term often used by computer professionals and manufacturers to refer to the person who uses the final service or product

End-user language
Language which enables programs to be written by an end user without any programming expertise

Ergonomics
The study of people and equipment in the working environment to provide satisfying and safe, as well as efficient and effective, working conditions. Often used to mean the physical design of equipment

Execute
To initiate and carry out an instruction or a complete routine or programme

Expert system
A system programmed in a logic language to follow the 'human reasoning' used by an expert to deduce certain findings, reached through a judgement based on experience, which has been distilled into the program (see LISP, PROLOG)

Field
The basic structural element in a file; a number of fields go to form a record and records are grouped to form files

Fifth generation
A range of computer architectures and capabilities designed for ease and naturalness of use as its prime objective; originated with a report in 1981 for the Japanese government

File
Information organised into an interrelated set of records, such as a student file or product file

File processing
A form of data management where information is structured into separate

files; this is more inefficient and inflexible than database management systems where the same data item can form part of many different files and data structures

Firmware

Software stored in hardwired form

Flexible manufacturing

Application where a number of machine tools and NC machines are controlled by a central computer; the production process can be changed by altering the control program rather than re-engineering machine tools

Flowchart

A graphical representation of the structure of a system, software, file or database (see Structured design)

Forward/backward chaining

An expert system normally works in one of two ways (though some do, in fact, use a combination of both)

Systems which work back through supporting evidence to establish the truth (or degree of truth) of a previously selected conclusion or 'goal' are said to be backward chaining or backward reasoning

Systems which start by establishing the status of evidence in order to select the 'goal' which follows from them are said to be forward chaining or forward reasoning

Frames

A method of storing knowledge. It is much like a traditional data record, and stores facts known about a particular subject. Each of these facts may, however, be itself a frame, so a network of such frames is constructed which describes the relationships between the various attributes of the main subject

Front-end processor
A system which removes some of the processing load from a central computer, typically handling communications co-ordination functions before the data is sent to the central system for processing

Fuzzy logic
Ways of reasoning that can cope with uncertain or partial information; characteristic of human thinking and many expert systems

Half-duplex
A communications link which allows data transmission in two directions, but not at the same time

Hard disk
A rigid magnetic oxide-coated disk with higher capacity than a floppy disk and held in a cartridge container

Hardware
The physical equipment of a computer system

Hardwired
Fixed electronic circuit patterns (see Microcode)

Heuristics
Methods of solving problems through successive 'trial-and-error' attempts at a solution, rather than by a predetermined algorithm; simple 'rules of thumb' or arbitrary figures of merit used to derive a conclusion from (sometimes incomplete or uncertain) evidence

High-level language
A programming language designed to match the information processing needs of the application; uses commands and statement structures similar to a restricted form of a natural language (see Low-level language)

Induction   The process of using a set of example situations to generate the implicit rule governing them

Inference engine   An expert system normally comprises two main sections: the knowledge base and the inference engine

                                  The knowledge base holds the knowledge about a particular topic in the form of facts ('John is Mary's father') and relationships ('A grandfather is the father of someone's father')

                                  The inference engine uses this knowledge to infer new knowledge by questioning the user and interpreting the appropriate rules of relationship

Informatics   Used synonymously with information technology; anglicised version of the French informatique, which is more the equivalent of data processing

Information management   The co-ordination of all information services in an organisation

Information retrieval   The use of a computer to search and extract information from a database

Information technology   The devices and techniques used to store, process, manage, transmit and communicate information; encompasses various technologies such as computing, microelectronics and tele-communications

Input   Information entered into a computer system for processing; the act of entering data

Installation   The location of the main computer hardware

Instruction set	The basic machine code operations provided by a particular computer architecture; each instruction initiates and performs a processing action once it has been decoded in the control unit
Instructions per second	Measurement of the power of a processor
Integer	A whole number (1,2,3. . . , etc)
Integrated circuit	Circuits composed of many transistors which have been reduced in size and placed together in a single physical element, typically into a silicon chip
Intelligent systems	The subject of machine intelligence is extremely contentious (it is, after all, difficult to reach agreement on what constitutes human intelligence!). What we mean here are those systems which display a behaviour similar to that one would expect from a human expert, though over only a narrow field of expertise
Intelligent terminal	A device which incorporates its own computing power
Interactive	An application where the user is involved in a continuous dialogue with the system
Interface	The junction between two devices, software modules or other elements involved in the operation of a computer
Interpreter	A program that translates a high-level language program into machine code statement by statement, rather than by analysing the complete program at once, as a compiler would do; typically used with an interactive language like BASIC

Interrupt	When the control unit stops processing to handle some external need, such as performing an I/O task
Key	One or more characters within an information structure used to identify the whole structure, for example the name field in a student file
Keyboard	Means of typing input to a computer; input part of a VDU
Knowledge base	See Inference engine
Knowledge elicitation	The translation of a human expert's knowledge into a form in which it can be operated on by the expert system
Knowledge engineer	The expert systems equivalent of the Systems Analyst. His job is to liaise with the human expert and to codify his knowledge in the form of facts and relationships for incorporation into a knowledge base
Linear programming	A mathematical technique which calculates the optimum solution to a problem involving many variables which interact within a framework of known constraints
LISP	A logic programming language
Local area network	A means of interlinking computers, terminals and other devices within a building
Logic operators	The basic actions and rules which determine the results used in Boolean algebra
Logic programming	A development of formal logic principles similar to the way expert systems reach conclusions by following logical inferences; suited to AI, expert sys-

tems, parallel processing, educational and other applications

Logical inferences per second

Measure of speed of a logic program like an expert system

Loop

A section of code repeated a given number of times

Low-level language

A programming language based on the format of the machine code of each architecture (see Assembly language)

Machine code

The numeric codes which form a computer's instruction set (see Low-level language)

Magnetic card

Cards coated with magnetic material for data storage; used with early word processors

Magnetic disk

Disks coated with magnetic material, similar to music records, used to store computer data

Magnetic media

Backing store which stores information as bits according to the magnetisation of tiny elements in the surface of the medium

Magnetic tape

Tapes coated with magnetic material, similar to tapes for a domestic tape recorder, used to store computer data

Main memory

Memory linked directly to the processor which holds programs and data required for immediate processing; sometimes regarded as part of the CPU

Mainframe

A computer with high capability, larger than other computers and generally provided with comprehensive applications and software support from the supplier

Management Information System (MIS)
A range of computing services which provide management and administration staff with timely and accurate information and aids to assist carrying out their work (see Decision support system)

Memory
Synonymous with computer storage but usually used in relation to main memory

Menu
A form of user/system interaction where the user selects an action from a menu of options

Microcode
Code used in a microprogram to turn a machine's instruction set into the appropriate signals to implement machine code; a microcoded instruction set can be altered whereas a hardwired implementation is fixed

Microcomputer
A complete computer; the smallest and cheapest computers available commercially

Microprocessor
A processing device on a chip

Microprogram
See Microcode

Minicomputer
A computer generally between a microcomputer and maxi/mainframe in price and performance, although demarcation between categories is fuzzy; often packaged as part of a small business system, word processor or intelligent terminal

Modelling
Software which simulates a system by manipulating a number of variables

	which interact with each other; can answer "What if . . .?" questions to predict behaviour of the modelled system depending on how the variables are altered (see Decision support system)
Module	A self-contained hardware or software unit which links with other modules to form a complete system (see Structured design)
Mouse	A device which moves the cursor on a screen in the same direction that the mouse is moved on a flat surface
Multifunction workstation	A workstation from which a variety of electronic office functions can be carried out
Multiprogramming	The ability to run more than one program at a time in the same computer
Natural language	A language, like English, used by people
Network	The interlinking of many computers, terminals and other devices by telecommunications links according to a structured architecture and agreed protocols for communication
Non-procedural language	A programming language designed for end users which matches applications processes rather than the algorithmic procedures of other programming languages
Non-volatile memory	Memory which retains information when its power supply is switched off
Number cruncher	Colloquialism for an application involving many complex calculations
Numerical control machine	A machine tool controlled by a program on a paper tape loop; a computer

	numerical control machine has more sophisticated control by computer software
Object code	The binary machine code produced by a compiler, assembler or interpreter after translating the source program
Off-line	Activities related to computer tasks carried out when the user, local computer, terminal or peripheral is not in direct communication with a central computer
On-line	Activity in direct communications with a computer, say by a terminal linked to a remote system
Operating system	Essential systems software which co-ordinates and controls the scheduling of work on the system and the use of the system's resources
Operator	Person who supervises and carries out the necessary physical tasks (like loading magnetic media) and is involved in processing work on a computer system; a word processing operator is a secretarial function which consists primarily of typing on a word processor
Optical Character Recognition (OCR)	Input method which automatically recognises printed characters
Output	The results of computer processing which could, for example, be presented on a VDU display or on a printer
Package software	Software which performs an applications task and which can be bought as a complete system

Parallel processing
A computer architecture, such as an array processor, which allows many processors to work on the same problem simultaneously

Parameter
A variable in a program or procedure which can be given a specific value for a given run or implementation of a program or to tailor packaged software to a specific user environment

Peripheral
Input, output and backing store devices which form part of a computer system

Personal computer
A microcomputer whose main application is for personal use rather than for corporate problem solving

Personal computing
A capability provided on a terminal in a computer network which offers similar functions to a personal computer

Portability
The ability to move a program from one computer to another; one objective of high level languages

Procedure
Part of a program which performs a specific task or calculation; an algorithm or subroutine

Process control
Application of a computer to monitor and automatically control a production process

Processor
Hardware unit which performs arithmetic and logic operations, controls the sequence of processing and co-ordinates input, output and storage activities (see Central Processing Unit, Parallel processing)

Production rules
Ways of representing knowledge in the form of IF (condition) THEN (result) rules

Program

A sequence of detailed instructions stored in a computer which automatically controls the actions of the hardware

PROLOG

A logic programming language

Protocols

A well-defined set of rules and conventions; agreed protocols must be used to provide compatibility across communications links

Relational database

A database management technique which relies on creating various relationships between basic data elements which are stored as tables with rows and columns

Robot

A computer-controlled machine which carries out some human-like physical movements; typically used on a production line to carry out a repetitive action involving limited physical arm and hand manipulations

Rules

These form part of the knowledge base of most expert systems. They define relationships between facts (or other rules), and are normally in the form of production rules

Semantic

The meaning of a language. A semantic program error is a fault in the program logic although the syntax may be correct

Semantic net

A way of representing knowledge in the form of a linked network, in which nodes represent concepts, and the arcs linking the nodes represent the relationships between them

Semiconductor

A substance, such as silicon, halfway between a conductor and insulator in allowing the flow of electronic current; suited to the construction of transistors

Set-down knowledge   Knowledge which already exists in a form suitable for incorporation into a knowledge base. This covers, for example, legal procedures and instruction manuals

Simulation   To represent the behaviour of one system by another, often using mathematical and modelling techniques which can be implemented by software; emulation is a form of simulation in which one system actually behaves like another rather than predicting how it might behave

Smart   Synonymous with intelligent, as in intelligent terminal

Software   Generic term for computer programs which are stored in and control the operation of hardware (see Firmware)

Software engineering   Techniques and aids which make software development, testing, amendment and enhancement a systematic and predictable process; structured design is an example of a software engineering method

Solid state   Devices, such as memories, which have transistors and integrated circuits as their active elements, without valves or mechanical components

Source code   Software in the language written by the user before it has been translated into machine-coded object form

Spooling   A technique to improve efficiency by writing printed output first to a magnetic media and then transferring it to a printer or other slower output device later, when the processor is engaged in other activities; also known as off-lining

Stand-alone

A computer-based system or device which can operate independently from any other computing resource

Stand-by

A duplicate computer or component to provide a back-up to ensure high availability of the system

Structured design

A systematic and well-documented approach to design which emphasises the use of modules within a framework that clearly identifies the necessary applications processes; structured design charts differ from flowcharts, which relate more to program rather than applications processes

Structured programming

Techniques of program design and implementation with similar objectives to structured design

Subroutine

Program code which performs a specific task and can be used by or incorporated in other programs

Symbolic address

Using a name rather than a number to identify a memory location

Syntax

The formal grammatical and spelling rules of a language (see Semantic)

Systems analyst

A skilled job function responsible for analysing an information management requirement and preparing a detailed specification from which programs can be developed

Systems software   Software, such as an operating system, concerned primarily with co-ordinating and controlling hardware and communications resources rather than applications tasks

Terminal   A device used for input, output and communications with a computer over telecommunications links

Text processing   Computer-based handling of information primarily in textual form, such as memos, reports and publications

Time sharing   A system which handles many on-line terminals simultaneously

Top-down design   A design approach which starts with the most general concepts or objectives and subdivides them into greater levels of detail within a structured framework

Transistor   A small electronic device which can act as a switch or amplifier and can be built into integrated circuits for computer processors and memories

Tuple   A structure containing two or more values (2-tuple, 3-tuple, etc). In effect it is a data record relating associated pieces of information. For instance, a 2-tuple could be 'Temperature – 40' or 'Length – 50'

Unconditional branch   A branch which transfers control automatically to the position in the program indicated by a label in the branch instruction

User   General term for the person, group or organisation operating the computer to perform an applications task

User friendly   Appealing to a user with no previous computing expertise

User/system interaction   Term for what is sometimes called man/machine communications or interface; the aspects of human factors engineering and ergonomics concerned with the techniques of communication between the user and the computer system

Value-added network   A network which provides information services (like electronic mail and viewdata) in addition to basic telecommunications transmission and switching capabilities

Variable   An entity which can assume different values; used in program procedures and to specify data areas which can take new values for each program run or can change during a run

Very Large Scale Integration (VLSI)   Measure of the circuit density of a chip, greater than Large Scale Integration; could be measured in millions of gates per chip

Visual Display Unit   A device with a TV-like display screen and associated keyboard

Voice recognition   Input by direct human speech which is automatically analysed by a computer

Voice response   Computer output in the form of speech

von Neumann architecture   An architecture built around the concept of a sequential central processing unit; named after computer pioneer John von Neumann

Word   A set of bits handled as a basic storage unit; can be of different bit lengths on different architectures

Word processing   Application of computing to the typing process; can be carried out by a purpose-built word processor or a software package on a general purpose computer (see Text processing)

Word processor   A device purpose-built for word and text processing applications

Workstation   A device (such as a VDU or word processor) or desk incorporating a number of devices from which people carry out work using electronic information handling techniques

Index of Expert Systems, Shells and Other Software Referred to in Text

General Index

Acorn	55, 61, 62, 78
AFIAS	150
AGAT micro	58-59
AI	
(see artificial intelligence)	
AI Ltd	40
Aiso, Hideo	49
Altos Computer Systems	68
Alvey, John	33
Alvey programme	23, 25, 27, 33-34, 35
American Association of	
Artificial Intelligence	20
Amstrad	62
Apple	60. 61
Applied Computer Techniques	23
Applied Expert Systems	114
architecture of expert systems	130-132
Aristotle	26
artificial intelligence	16-17, 18-28, 31-39,
(see also expert systems)	42-43, 48, 77-81, 82, 85
Association for Computing	
Machinery (ACM)	19
AT & T	61, 68-69, 176
Australia	78-79, 162
Babauskis, Alex	79